# SEVEN
## BLESSINGS
### OF THE
*Passover*

# SEVEN
## BLESSINGS

## OF THE
# *Passover*

## STEVE MUNSEY

Clarion Call Marketing

SEVEN BLESSINGS
OF THE PASSOVER

Published by
Clarion Call Marketing, Inc.
Dallas, Texas

All Scripture quotations, unless otherwise indicated, are taken from the *King James Version.*

Scripture quotations marked (NKJV) are taken from the *New King James Version.* Copyright © 1982 by Thomas Nelson, Inc. Used by permission. All rights reserved.

Scripture quotations marked (NRSV) are taken from the *New Revised Standard Version of the Bible,* copyright 1989 by the Division of Christian Education of the National Council of the Churches of Christ in the USA. Used by permission. All rights reserved.

Scripture quotations marked (GW) are taken from *God's Word,* a copyrighted work of God's Word to the Nations. Quotations are used by permission. Copyright 1995 by God's Word to the Nations. All rights reserved.

Scripture quotations marked (NIV) are taken from the *Holy Bible, New International Version,* NIV®. Copyright © 1973, 1978, 1984 by International Bible Society. Used by permission of Zondervan Publishing House. All rights reserved.

Scripture quotations marked (NLT) are taken from the *Holy Bible, New Living Translation,* copyright © 1996. Used by permission of Tyndale House Publishers, Inc., Wheaton, Illinois 60189. All rights reserved.

ISBN: 1-59574-059-7

*Printed in the United States of America*
2005—First Edition

10 9 8 7 6 5 4 3

# CONTENTS

# INTRODUCTION

## WHAT IS PASSOVER?

Where did it come from?

Why is it important to Christians?

More to the point, what does an ancient Hebrew feast called Passover have to do with Christian believers nearly thirty-five hundred years after the feast began?

Here is a brief history, leading to the reason why I feel God told me to write a book with the specific title *Seven Blessings of Passover*:

- The events that led to the Passover were probably the most dramatic in all the Old Testament. The children of Israel were living in slavery in Egypt. Pharaoh was a severe taskmaster, and the Israelites seemed to have no hope of getting out. It was during that time that God spoke to Moses from a burning bush in the desert. Dry and without sap, the bush should have burned up quickly, but that didn't happen. Moses turned to observe this remarkable sight, and out of the bush God spoke to him: *And the angel of the LORD appeared unto him in a flame of fire out of the midst of a bush: and he looked, and, behold, the bush burned with fire, and the bush was not consumed* (Exodus 3:2).

- God designed seven feasts for the Israelites (Leviticus 23). These feasts were God's own holy days, and there were specific instructions given for their observance. The Hebrew word translated feasts means "appointed times." God Himself orchestrated the sequence and time of each of these feasts.

- Three times a year the Israelites were to appear together before the Lord. The word of God strictly instructed them that they must not appear before Him without an offering.

Deuteronomy 16:16 states, *"And they shall not appear before the LORD empty-handed"* (NKJV).

❧ The first feast of the Lord is Passover. It is the foundational feast. While the Jewish people have celebrated the Passover annually since the time of Moses, in reality, there was only one Passover. It occurred sometime around 1446 BC in Egypt.[1] It was at that time of the Exodus that a lamb was sacrificed and the blood was applied to each door post and gate. When this was done in faith and obedience to God's command, that home was "passed over," and the life of the firstborn was spared. All succeeding observances over the centuries have been memorials of that one and only first Passover.

❧ God is a covenant-keeping God. What His mouth speaks, His right arm of power causes to be performed. Thus, the Israelites, as unattractive and undesirable as they may have appeared at that time, were still His people. He saw their plight, He observed their many afflictions, and He decided it was time for them to leave after more than four hundred years in Egypt.

❧ It would be almost impossible to overstate the exodus from Egypt. Even Hollywood, with all its hype and special effects, did not exaggerate the reality of this miraculous event. God had hardened Pharaoh's heart so he wouldn't let the children of Israel leave his country. Plague after plague came upon the Egyptians without his giving in and letting them go. Finally, Moses announced that the firstborn of each home in Egypt would be taken by the death angel where there was no blood on the doorpost. At this terrible event, Pharaoh decided the children of Israel could leave. All those slaves with their possessions walked past the Pyramids and the Great Sphinx to freedom.

❧ God established the Passover as a feast to be kept forever: *"It is the LORD's Passover... so this day shall be to you a memorial; and you shall keep it as a feast to the LORD throughout your generations. You shall keep it as a feast by an everlasting ordinance"* (Exodus 12:11, 14, NKJV). This feast was established for the Israelites in the time of their flight from Egypt, but it also was consecrated as an appointed holy time each year throughout both the Old and the New Testaments. I will explain more about this in chapter 2.

🥢 In AD 325, the Roman emperor Constantine stopped the Passover as a church practice. Since that time, the holy convocations (the feasts) have not been observed by Christians.

Lost through the centuries since AD 325 is the fact that God promised seven major blessings to those who observe His feasts. Specifically, those obedient in the Passover Feast were promised seven blessings—seven specific, supernatural blessings.

However, for nearly seventeen centuries, these powerful truths have been mostly ignored and even rejected by Christians. That must change! The time for change is now. There is too much at stake.

For years God has been stirring me to write this book, to tell people how their lives would change dramatically when they restored the Passover offering. Increasingly, I have been reminded that God sets schedules and time boundaries, especially for His feasts and blessings. He is poised to pour out these blessings upon your life. As you read this book you will learn how to unleash these Passover blessings in your life today.

It is my prayer that God will use the pages of this book to revolutionize your life and will pour out more blessings than you ever dreamed possible. More than anything, I pray that you will understand why God wants you to receive the seven blessings.

# PART ONE

*Passover*

# CHAPTER 1

# THE PASSOVER

WITHOUT BELABORING THE POINT, let me say that the feasts of Israel, beginning with Passover, were built upon the foundation of God's blood covenant with mankind. This goes back to Adam and Eve, who lived in a perfect world, blameless, and without guilt. The first man and woman knew God intimately. They walked with Him and fellowshiped with Him regularly. Then they rebelled through a sin of disobedience. They ate from the Tree of Knowledge of Good and Evil. This is more than a mere allegory. It is the basis for all that follows for mankind, as presented throughout both the Old and New Testaments.

In the midst of God's judgment for their disobedience, however, came a wonderful promise of redemption through the shed blood of Jesus Christ. God cursed Satan, in the form of a serpent, who had tempted Adam and Eve into disobedience: *"And I will put enmity between thee and the woman, and between thy seed and her seed; it shall bruise thy head, and thou shalt bruise his heel"* (Genesis 3:15).

As soon as God gave this first promise of Christ's deliverance, God immediately offered the first blood sacrifice. After they sinned, Adam and Eve ran from God's presence to avoid letting Him see their nakedness. God selected animals—some scholars suggest a lamb—and with the skins from the slain animals, apparently still moist with blood, He covered their sin.

And from that time forward, there were numerous examples

of the blood-red trail of the blood covenant that attempted to cover mankind's disobedience.

Then look at Noah. The first action he took, once the flood waters subsided and his family was able to disembark from the ark, was to offer a blood covenant with the Lord: *"And Noah builded an altar unto the LORD; and took of every clean beast, and of every clean fowl, and offered burnt offerings on the altar"* (Genesis 8:20).

Abraham, the father of all nations, was chosen by God to enter a covenant that would literally change the course of history. That covenant involved the shedding of blood:

> *And when Abram was ninety years old and nine, the LORD appeared to Abram, and said unto him, I am the Almighty God; walk before me, and be thou perfect. And I will make my covenant between me and thee, and will multiply thee exceedingly. And Abram fell on his face: and God talked with him, saying, As for me, behold, my covenant is with thee, and thou shalt be a father of many nations. Neither shall thy name any more be called Abram, but thy name shall be Abraham; for a father of many nations have I made thee. And I will make thee exceeding fruitful, and I will make nations of thee, and kings shall come out of thee. And I will establish my covenant between me and thee and thy seed after thee in their generations for an everlasting covenant, to be a God unto thee, and to thy seed after thee. And I will give unto thee, and to thy seed after thee, the land wherein thou art a stranger, all the land of Canaan, for an everlasting possession; and I will be their God.*
>
> *And God said unto Abraham, Thou shalt keep my covenant therefore, thou, and thy seed after thee in their generations. This is my covenant, which ye shall keep, between me and you and thy seed after thee; Every man child among you shall be circumcised.*
> (Genesis 17:1-10)

Abraham offered his son Isaac as a test of his willingness to obey the God with whom he had entered this covenant. God spared Isaac's life at the last moment by providing a ram as a blood sacrifice:

*And the angel of the LORD called unto him out of heaven, and said, Abraham, Abraham: and he said, Here am I. And he said, Lay not thine hand upon the lad, neither do thou any thing unto him: for now I know that thou fearest God, seeing thou hast not withheld thy son, thine only son from me. And Abraham lifted up his eyes, and looked, and behold behind him a ram caught in a thicket by his horns: and Abraham went and took the ram, and offered him up for a burnt offering in the stead of his son. And Abraham called the name of that place Jehovahjireh: as it is said to this day, In the mount of the LORD it shall be seen.* (Genesis 22:11-14)

Jacob, Isaac's son and Abraham's grandson, obviously understood the necessity and absolute value of a blood covenant, for we find in Genesis 35:11-12: *"And God said unto him, I am God Almighty: be fruitful and multiply; a nation and a company of nations shall be of thee, and kings shall come out of thy loins; and the land which I gave Abraham and Isaac, to thee I will give it, and to thy seed after thee will I give the land."*

Not long after God delivered Moses the Ten Commandments, the leader of the children of Israel brought the people together and offered young bulls as a blood sacrifice: *"And Moses took the blood, and sprinkled it on the people, and said, Behold the blood of the covenant, which the LORD hath made with you concerning all these words"* (Exodus 24:8).

Many more accounts of the blood covenant are found throughout the Old Testament, but perhaps none more graphically presented than through the feasts of Israel, especially the Passover and what led to God establishing that feast. In these next few pages, I pray God will reveal even more of His wonderful Old Covenant and New Covenant plan to you as we move toward spotlighting the seven blessings of the Passover.

## Captivity

The events that led to the Passover were probably the most dramatic in all the Old Testament. The book of Genesis relates how Joseph was sold into slavery, taken to Egypt, endured great hardship, and was eventually given a top position in the nation's government because of God's favor on his life.

Through his influence and administration, Egypt flourished. His family, still in Canaan, heard about abundant grain there and the older brothers—the same ones who had sold him for thirty pieces of silver—came to obtain grain during a seven-year famine that stretched throughout the region. In due time, Joseph revealed that he was their long-lost brother, forgave his siblings, and invited the entire family to live in Egypt.

Years passed. Joseph and his brothers died, and the children of Israel multiplied in the land of Egypt. They held important positions and played an important role in the political, cultural, and economic life of the country. Pharaoh died as well and his predecessor apparently had little sympathy or love for the children of Israel.

It is generally accepted as historical fact that approximately thirty-five hundred years ago, the Hebrews were enslaved by the Egyptians under the rule of the Pharaoh Ramses II. Forgetting what Joseph had done for Egypt, the new pharaoh decided to take action against the growing influence and numbers of the children of Israel. The "foreigners" were brutally forced to build cities, erect monuments, construct roads, work in the quarries, and hew stones or make bricks and tiles. However, according to biblical and historical records, the more the Egyptians oppressed them, the more the children of Israel increased and multiplied.

When it seemed the children of Israel could no longer endure their terrible suffering and persecution, their cries for help pierced the heavens. God remembered His covenant with Abraham, Isaac, and Jacob and delivered their descendants from bondage.

You see, God is a covenant-keeping God. What His mouth speaks, His right arm of power causes to be performed. Thus, the Israelites, as unattractive and undesirable as they may have appeared at that time, were still His people. He saw their plight, He observed their many afflictions, and He decided it was time for them to leave—after more than four hundred years in Egypt.

## The Plagues

In a gruesome attempt to avoid the growing multitude of Hebrews, Pharaoh gave an order that all newly born male Hebrew descendents be killed. Only daughters should be permitted to live. According to the book of Exodus, however, Moses, the child of Jewish parents, was saved from the edict when he was found by Pharaoh's daughter and raised in the household of Egypt's ruler. He fled the country after killing a man and spent forty years in the desert as a shepherd before the burning bush experience and God's call to return to Egypt.

God instructed Moses to go to Pharaoh and demand the freedom of His people. Moses returned, and, with the help of his brother Aaron, issued repeated pleas to Pharaoh to "let my people go." Moses was eighty years old and his brother eighty-three when they entered the palace of Pharaoh.

Pharaoh haughtily refused, saying that he had never heard of the God of the Israelites. The pleas were ignored. Moses warned the pharaoh that God would send punishments on the people of Egypt, in increased severity, if the Israelites were not allowed to leave. Repeatedly, the Pharaoh ignored Moses's request for freedom. As a result, God unleashed a series of ten horrible plagues upon the nation of Egypt:

## 1. Blood (Exodus 7)

When Pharaoh persisted in his refusal to liberate the children of Israel, Moses and Aaron warned that God would punish the Egyptians. First, the waters of the land were to be turned into blood.

Moses walked with Aaron to the brink of the river. There Aaron raised his staff, smote the water, and the streams were turned into blood. All the people of Egypt and the king himself watched as their sacred river changed from a river, famed for its delicious taste, into a smelly mess of dying fish and filth. Man and beast suffered horrible thirst. Yet Pharaoh would not give in.

## 2. Frogs (Exodus 8)

After another warning, the second plague began. Aaron stretched his hand over the waters of Egypt and frogs swarmed over every inch of land. Can you imagine? Wherever the Egyptians turned, there were slimy bodies and the croakings of frogs.

Pharaoh became frightened, and he asked Moses and Aaron to pray to God to remove the frogs, promising to free the Jewish people at once. As soon as the frogs disappeared, he again broke his promise and refused to let the children of Israel go.

## 3. Lice (Exodus 8)

God told Aaron to smite the dust of the earth with his staff. Instantly Egypt crawled with lice. Man and beast suffered untold misery from this terrible plague. Although even a casual observer could have recognized it as God's punishment, Pharaoh steeled his heart and remained steadfast in his determination to keep the children of Israel in bondage.

## 4. Flies (Exodus 8)

The fourth plague to trouble the Egyptians consisted of hordes of filthy flies roving all over the country. Only the land of Goshen where the children of Israel dwelt was immune from this plague, as with the other affliction.

Again Pharaoh promised faithfully to let the Hebrews go out into the desert on the condition that they would not go too far. Moses prayed to God, and the flies disappeared.

As soon as they had gone, Pharaoh withdrew his promise and refused Moses's demand.

### 5. Livestock Diseased (Exodus 9)

God then sent a disease that killed most of the Egyptians' livestock. How the people must have grieved when they saw their prized animals stricken at the word of Moses. These animals, many of them looked upon as gods, died throughout the land. Meanwhile, the word undoubtedly spread that the Hebrew animals remained unhurt. Still, Pharaoh's heart was hardened, and he would not let the Israelites go.

### 6. Boils (Exodus 9)

Then came the sixth plague. Nasty boils appeared on man and beast throughout the land. This must have been so agonizing and repugnant that it filled the people of Egypt with terror and distress. More of the same from Pharaoh—he didn't budge.

### 7. Hail (Exodus 9)

Moses announced to the king that a hailstorm of unprecedented violence was to sweep the land. When Moses stretched forth his staff, the hail pelted down with such violence that man and beast who were exposed to the icy fury died on the spot. Egypt was devastated. The land of Goshen, by contrast, was untouched by the ravages of the storm. Then Pharaoh sent for Moses and acknowledged his sins, but when the storm ceased, Pharaoh's heart remained hardened.

### 8. Locusts (Exodus 10)

The next time Moses and Aaron came before Pharaoh, he appeared somewhat relenting and tried to work out a compromise (all Hebrew men could leave, but the women, children, and possessions must remain in Egypt). Moses and Aaron did not accept his offer, of course, which left Pharaoh furious. As soon as Moses left the palace, swarms of locusts blocked the sun, devouring everything that had escaped the previous plagues.

Again Pharaoh relented, but when relief came Pharaoh's hard heart returned and the people of Israel remained in bondage.

## 9. Darkness (Exodus 10)

The ninth plague followed, and Egypt was enveloped in a thick darkness. The Egyptians were naturally gripped with fear. Light was only in Goshen, where the children of Israel dwelt.

Again Pharaoh tried to haggle with Moses and Aaron, promising to allow the children of Israel to leave if their flocks and herds remained in Egypt. Moses and Aaron refused to accept nothing less than complete freedom for all of the men, women, children, and their possessions.

Pharaoh became angry, ordering Moses and Aaron to leave and warning them with a death sentence if they appeared in front of him again.

Moses told him they would not need to see him again, for God was going to send one more plague over Egypt which would force Pharaoh to give his unconditional permission for the children of Israel to leave Egypt.

## 10. Death of the Firstborn (Exodus 11—12)

When the final plague was announced, God declared, *"About midnight will I go out into the midst of Egypt: And all the firstborn in the land of Egypt shall die"* (Exodus 11:4-5).

At the same time, the Lord told Moses He was about to give His people a new beginning. God said:

> *And the LORD spake unto Moses and Aaron in the land of Egypt, saying, This month shall be unto you the beginning of months: it shall be the first month of the year to you. Speak ye unto all the congregation of Israel, saying, In the tenth day of this month they shall take to them every man a lamb, according to the house of*

*their fathers, a lamb for an house: And if the household be too little for the lamb, let him and his neighbour next unto his house take it according to the number of the souls; every man according to his eating shall make your count for the lamb. Your lamb shall be without blemish, a male of the first year: ye shall take it out from the sheep, or from the goats: And ye shall keep it up until the fourteenth day of the same month: and the whole assembly of the congregation of Israel shall kill it in the evening. And they shall take of the blood, and strike it on the two side posts and on the upper door post of the houses, wherein they shall eat it. And they shall eat the flesh in that night, roast with fire, and unleavened bread; and with bitter herbs they shall eat it. Eat not of it raw, nor sodden at all with water, but roast with fire; his head with his legs, and with the purtenance thereof. And ye shall let nothing of it remain until the morning; and that which remaineth of it until the morning ye shall burn with fire. And thus shall ye eat it; with your loins girded, your shoes on your feet, and your staff in your hand; and ye shall eat it in haste: it is the LORD's passover.*

*For I will pass through the land of Egypt this night, and will smite all the firstborn in the land of Egypt, both man and beast; and against all the gods of Egypt I will execute judgment: I am the LORD. And the blood shall be to you for a token upon the houses where ye are: and when I see the blood, I will pass over you, and the plague shall not be upon you to destroy you, when I smite the land of Egypt. And this day shall be unto you for a memorial; and ye shall keep it a feast to the LORD throughout your generations.*
(Exodus 12:1-14)

Notice in chapter 12 that the children of Israel were instructed to keep the lamb until the fourteenth day of the month and to kill it in the evening (verse 6). Before eating, they were to *"take of the blood, and strike it on the two side posts and on the upper door post of the houses*" (verse 7). God told them to eat all of the lamb, for "*it is the LORD's passover*" (verse 11).

Why was shedding the blood, eating the lamb, and placing blood on the doorframes so significant? On the same night, God said He would pass through the land and smite the firstborn in the land of Egypt (verse 12). The lamb's shed blood became their salvation.

At midnight, God unleashed the plague of the firstborn "*and there was a great cry in Egypt; for there was not a house where there was not one dead*" (verse 30). The Egyptians were "*urgent upon the people, that they might send them out of the land in haste; for they said, We be all dead men*" (verse 33).

Upwards to 3 million Jews were in captivity, yet that night a divine miracle was about to take place. They were visited by the power of God. Because they ate the lamb, supernatural health was theirs. When they walked out of Egypt they were a healthy and healed people: "*There was not one feeble person among their tribes*" (Psalm 105:37).

What brought about this strength and well-being? It was through the sacrificial blood of the covenant, highly mindful of healing that flows from our Savior's punishment, for it is "*with his stripes we are healed*" (Isaiah 53:5).

Passover, or the Hebrew word *pesach*, literally means "protection," and it comes from the explicit instructions given by God to Moses on the night the angel of death passed over those homes marked with blood.

## The Exodus

Even after Pharaoh finally relented and offered the Jews their release, their liberation was far from over. Pharaoh's army chased them through the desert toward the Red Sea. When the Jews reached the sea they were trapped, since the sea blocked their escape.

A miracle happened! In obedience to God's command, Moses stretched forth his rod and the Red Sea parted. The entire multitude of Israelites crossed to the other side. The Bible even mentions that they crossed the seabed, but that the land was dry. Imagine! And as soon as they reached the other side, Moses lowered his staff, and the supernatural seawalls on either side collapsed, trapping Pharaoh's army in a watery grave. As the children of Israel watched the Red Sea sweep over the Egyptian army, they realized, above all else, they were finally free. The Passover Feast celebrates this miraculous history.

## God's Covenant

I was studying this wonderful passage many years ago, and the Lord showed me something that thrilled me in a life-changing way. God's covenant with Abraham, made centuries before, was the reason for Israel's exodus from slavery in Egypt.

> *And it came to pass in process of time, that the king of Egypt died: and the children of Israel sighed by reason of the bondage, and they cried, and their cry came up unto God by reason of the bondage. And God heard their groaning, and God remembered his covenant with Abraham, with Isaac, and with Jacob. And God looked upon the children of Israel, and God had respect unto them.* (Exodus 2:23-25)

Other versions of the Bible translate that final passage this way: *"and God was concerned about them."* Isn't that amazing?

As Moses led the children of Israel into the desert, the covenant was the binding force that held the multitude together. When he received the Ten Commandments and words of God's law, Moses quickly moved to reinstate the blood covenant between God and His chosen people. Moses told the people what God had instructed him to do: *"And Moses came and told the people all the words of the LORD, and all the judgments: and all the people answered with one voice, and said, All the words which the LORD hath said will we do"* (Exodus 24:3).

This declaration and subsequent approval was an all-important step in establishing a new blood covenant between God and His people. Soon afterward, God established the feasts, which were celebrations of the time He brought the Hebrews out of Egypt.

## Three Feast Seasons— Seven Feasts

As recorded in Leviticus 23, God instructed the children of Israel to hold seven holy gatherings[1] each year and established them on the Jewish calendar so the people would need to travel to Jerusalem three times a year. The Jewish calendar is based on the lunar cycle, so it is different from our Gregorian or Julian calendar, both based on the solar cycles. The Jewish calendar is eleven days shorter than a solar-based calendar. To reconcile the difference between our solar-based calendar (365.25 days) and the lunar year (354 days), the Jewish calendar is based upon a nineteen-year cycle in which the third, sixth, eighth, eleventh, fourteenth, seventeenth, and nineteenth years are leap years. It is for this reason that the feasts do not fall on the same day each year of the calendars we use today.

These three feast seasons were called Passover, Pentecost, and Tabernacles, which represented the three major links between God and His covenant children. These feasts also relate directly to Israel's agricultural seasons.

### Passover

The first feast season, Passover, included the Feasts of Passover, Unleavened Bread and Firstfruits. These first three feasts occurred over eight days during the spring of the year. Referred together as "Passover," the purpose of this brief season was to teach the children of Israel how to find and enter God's true rest. The Bible commanded that the various feasts were to be kept in their appointed seasons: *"Let the children of Israel also keep the passover at his appointed season. In the fourteenth day of this month, at even, ye shall keep it in his appointed season: according to all the rites of it, and according to all the ceremonies thereof, shall ye keep it"* (Numbers 9:2-3).

## Pentecost

The second season, Pentecost, was a single gathering. During this feast the Hebrews were taught explicitly how to receive and live in God's supernatural power. Originally called the Feast of Weeks, by New Testament times this feast was known by its Greek name, Pentecost.

## Tabernacles

The third season of feasts is collectively known as Tabernacles. This season included the Feast of Trumpets, Day of Atonement, and Feast of Tabernacles. Always the most glorious season of all and celebrated over twenty-one days in the fall of each year, the purpose of this season was to teach the children of Israel how to enter God's protection.

Each of these feasts were extremely significant times for the Hebrews, for they led the children of Israel and their descendents to honor God for what He had done in their lives. Even a first-time reader of the Old Testament account of the Exodus, Passover, and seven feasts cannot help but notice that the seven feasts given by God to the children of Israel were uniquely meaningful. These were God's own holy days, and specific instructions were given for their observance.

The first, Passover, was a foundational feast. Those who correctly observed this feast received supernatural blessings. Just as God did with the children of Israel, He is poised to pour out these seven blessings upon your life, as you will later see in chapter 3. First, however, in chapter 2 we will put to rest, once and for all, whether Christians should observe Passover.

# SHOULD CHRISTIANS CELEBRATE PASSOVER?

GOD DESIGNED SEVEN FEASTS for the Israelites (Leviticus 23). These feasts were God's own holy days, and there were specific instructions given for their observance. The Hebrew word translated "feasts" means "appointed times." The sequence and time of each of these feasts have been carefully orchestrated by God Himself.

The three feast seasons of Passover, Pentecost, and Tabernacles each represent the three major links between God and His covenant children. The seven great feasts of the Lord—Passover, Unleavened Bread, Firstfruits, Pentecost, Trumpets, Day of Atonement, and Tabernacles—all point backward to what God did to establish His covenant with the children of Israel. All likewise point to Christ the Savior. Because they all illuminate the supernatural truths and blessings that we can receive from observing these feasts, especially Passover, these feasts are filled with meaning for believers still today.

**The Feast of the Passover points to Christ our Passover:**

*"Purge out therefore the old leaven, that ye may be a new lump, as ye are unleavened. For even Christ our passover is sacrificed for us"* (1 Corinthians 5:7).

**The Feast of Unleavened Bread directs us toward Jesus, our Bread of Life:**

*"And Jesus said unto them, I am the bread of life: he that cometh to me shall never hunger; and he that believeth on me shall never thirst"* (John 6:35).

**The Feast of the Firstfruits guides us directly to the Savior:**

*But now is Christ risen from the dead, and become the first-fruits of them that slept. For since by man came death, by man came also the resurrection of the dead. For as in Adam all die, even so in Christ shall all be made alive. But every man in his own order: Christ the firstfruits; afterward they that are Christ's at his coming."* (1 Corinthians 15:20-23)

**The Feast of Pentecost specifically shows that Jesus sent the Holy Spirit to bear witness of the Savior during Pentecost:**

*And when the day of Pentecost was fully come, they were all with one accord in one place. And suddenly there came a sound from heaven as of a rushing mighty wind, and it filled all the house where they were sitting. And there appeared unto them cloven tongues like as of fire, and it sat upon each of them. And they were all filled with the Holy Ghost, and began to speak with other tongues, as the Spirit gave them utterance.* (Acts 2:1-4)

This fulfillment came as a direct result of Christ's own prophetic words given to His followers just before His ascension into heaven: *"But ye shall receive power, after that the Holy Ghost is come upon you: and ye shall be witnesses unto me both in Jerusalem, and in all Judaea, and in Samaria, and unto the uttermost part of the earth"* (Acts 1:8).

**The Feast of Trumpets reveals the soon-coming Savior.** We are to look for His appearance: *"For the Lord himself shall descend from heaven with a shout, with the voice of the archangel, and with the trump of God: and the dead in Christ shall rise first"* (1 Thessalonians 4:16).

**The Day of Atonement guides us to understand how the Word became flesh:**

> *But God commendeth his love toward us, in that, while we were yet sinners, Christ died for us. Much more then, being now justified by his blood, we shall be saved from wrath through him. For if, when we were enemies, we were reconciled to God by the death of his Son, much more, being reconciled, we shall be saved by his life. And not only so, but we also joy in God through our Lord Jesus Christ, by whom we have now received the atonement.*
>
> *Wherefore, as by one man sin entered into the world, and death by sin; and so death passed upon all men, for that all have sinned: (For until the law sin was in the world: but sin is not imputed when there is no law. Nevertheless death reigned from Adam to Moses, even over them that had not sinned after the similitude of Adam's transgression, who is the figure of him that was to come. But not as the offence, so also is the free gift. For if through the offence of one many be dead, much more the grace of God, and the gift by grace, which is by one man, Jesus Christ, hath abounded unto many.* (Romans 5:8-15)

**The Feast of Tabernacles shows us the Creator's plan to send His Son to establish fellowship with us as well as to establish His authority, ownership, and reign:** *"And the Word was made flesh, and dwelt among us, (and we beheld his glory, the glory as of the only begotten of the Father,) full of grace and truth"* (John 1:14).

Through each of the feasts, especially the Passover, it is clearly evident how all that follows in the Old Covenant pointed toward the Cross and beyond. After Calvary, the Savior is offering blessings beyond measure. That New Covenant will be featured in chapter 11.

Specifically, God established that the Passover was a feast that is to be kept forever (Exodus 12:14). This was not established only for the Israelites in the time of their flight from Egypt; this ordinance was a consecrated appointed (holy) time throughout both the Old and the New Testaments.

## From Passover to Easter

In AD 325, the emperor, Constantine, convened the Council of Nicea. He wanted to unite the many Christian groups throughout his kingdom. Many changes happened as a result, including:

- The date of the observance of Jesus's birth became December 25.

- The day of worship was moved from the Sabbath (Saturday) to the first day of each week (Sunday).

- The doctrine of the Trinity was confirmed as orthodox Christian belief.

- The Church of Rome was officially established.

One of the important teachings omitted from the Nicene Creed—as a result of the Nicene Council—was the observance of the "Hebrew" feasts. Some believe that Constantine had seen that God's people were blessed as a result of observing the feasts, beginning with Passover, and as a consequence, he stopped their adherence to God's command. It was after this time also that the word *Passover* came into disuse and was replaced by *Easter*.

Easter is generally understood to be named after the Babylonian goddess Ishtra, a pagan goddess of fertility. Even today these symbols of fertility are used in celebrating Easter—cute rabbits, dyed eggs, and new Sunday-best clothing all symbolize spring and the beginning of the growing season.

Please note that I am not implying that Christians, by enjoying the Easter season, are celebrating or worshiping the pagan goddess Ishtra. Constantine wanted to universalize the celebration throughout the Christian world, and since both the Passover season and the pagan celebrations happened during the same time of the year, it seemed simple enough to refer to the time as Easter. Christians clearly are celebrating the resurrection of Jesus Christ and not some pagan deity. However, erasing the Passover season and the blessings inherent in observing Passover has been tragic.

Technically, instead of Easter, we should still be celebrating the Passover season, part of which is the Feast of Firstfruits. Jesus arose during the Feast of Firstfruits. In 1 Corinthians 15:23, Paul even refers to "Christ the firstfruits." The real point of the feast was looking to the resurrection of the Messiah. Jesus, the Messiah, was our provision for spiritual welfare. Jesus, the Bread of Life, was raised on the first day of the Feast of Firstfruits, the last feast the Lord took part in while on earth.

Regardless, since AD 325, celebrating the Passover season and remainder of the holy convocations (the feasts) has not been a part of the church knowledge until these latter days.

## Reminder of Deliverance

Many Christians have been taught that Passover is an outdated Jewish observance done away with at Jesus's death and replaced by Easter, the commemoration of His resurrection. But why did Jesus Christ keep the Passover? Is there a connection between Passover and Christ's death? What does the Bible teach us about this most important observance kept by Jesus and the apostles?

In ancient Israel the first Passover was a time of deliverance, the rescuing of the Israelites from slavery in Egypt. The blood of the Passover lamb was smeared on the door posts of the residences of those Israelites who put their trust in God, and He promised to deliver them from harm (Exodus 12:13, 23). The Israelites were spared while the firstborn of the Egyptians were slain.

God ordained the Passover as a commanded feast: *"So this day shall be unto you for a memorial; and ye shall keep it a feast to the LORD throughout your generation; ye shall keep it a feast by an ordinance for ever"* (Exodus 12:14).

Much later, during the time of Christ, the observance of the New Testament Passover was revealed as the first step toward salvation. It reminds Christians not only of ancient Israel's deliverance from Egypt, but, more important, our deliverance from sin today. *"We know that our old self was crucified with him so that the body of sin might be destroyed, and we might no longer be enslaved to sin"* (Romans 6:6, NRSV).

The Passover is the first of the annual feasts commanded by God (Leviticus 23:5). Jesus knew this and kept the Passover with His disciples (Luke 22), showing that this is not a command to be taken lightly.

During His final Passover with His disciples, Jesus Christ introduced new symbols which commemorate Him as our Passover, who was sacrificed for us (1 Corinthians 5:7). Jesus said, after He had broken the unleavened bread and given it to His disciples, *"This is my body which is given for you: this do in remembrance of me"* (Luke 22:19).

The words to this old hymn reflect perfectly:

Christ our Redeemer died on the cross,
Died for the sinner, paid all his due;
Sprinkle your soul with the blood of the Lamb,
And I will pass, will pass over you.

Chiefest of sinners Jesus will save—
All He has promised, that He will do;
Wash in the fountain opened for sin,
And I will pass, will pass over you.

When I see the blood, When I see the blood,
When I see the blood, I will pass, I will pass over you.[1]

The Passover is an annual reminder that, through Christ's sacrifice, we have been set free from slavery to sin that we might serve God in righteousness (Romans 6:1-22).

## Jesus's Example

Jesus Christ observed the Passover. The Bible makes this clear in many passages, beginning with this glimpse into His childhood: *"Now his parents went to Jerusalem every year at the feast of the passover. And when he was twelve years old, they went up to Jerusalem after the custom of the feast"* (Luke 2:41-42).

There are numerous other examples:

*Ye know that after two days is the feast of the passover, and the Son of man is betrayed to be crucified.... Now the first day of the feast of unleavened bread the disciples came to Jesus, saying unto him, Where wilt thou that we prepare for thee to eat the passover?*

*And he said, Go into the city to such a man, and say unto him, The Master saith, My time is at hand; I will keep the passover at thy house with my disciples.*

*And the disciples did as Jesus had appointed them; and they made ready the passover.* (Matthew 26:2, 17-19)

*Now the feast of unleavened bread drew nigh, which is called the Passover....*

*Then came the day of unleavened bread, when the passover must be killed....*

*And they went, and found as he had said unto them: and they made ready the Passover....*

*And when the hour was come, he sat down, and the twelve apostles with him. And he said unto them, With desire I have desired to eat this passover with you before I suffer: For I say unto you, I will not any more eat thereof, until it be fulfilled in the kingdom of God.*

*And he took the cup, and gave thanks, and said, Take this, and divide it among yourselves: For I say unto you, I will not drink of the fruit of the vine, until the kingdom of God shall come.*

*And he took bread, and gave thanks, and brake it, and gave unto them, saying, This is my body which is given for you: this do in remembrance of me.*

*Likewise also the cup after supper, saying, This cup is the new testament in my blood, which is shed for you.* (Luke 22:1, 7, 13-20)

*And the Jews' passover was at hand, and Jesus went up to Jerusalem.... Now when he was in Jerusalem at the passover, in the feast day, many believed in his name, when they saw the miracles which he did.* (John 2:13, 23)

*For I have received of the Lord that which also I delivered unto you, That the Lord Jesus the same night in which he was betrayed took bread: And when he had given thanks, he brake it, and said, Take, eat: this is my body, which is broken for you: this do in remembrance of me. After the same manner also he took the cup, when he had supped, saying, This cup is the new testament in my blood: this do ye, as oft as ye drink it, in remembrance of me.*

*For as often as ye eat this bread, and drink this cup, ye do shew the Lord's death till he come.*

*Wherefore whosoever shall eat this bread, and drink this cup of the Lord, unworthily, shall be guilty of the body and blood of the Lord. But let a man examine himself, and so let him eat of that bread, and drink of that cup. For he that eateth and drinketh unworthily, eateth and drinketh damnation to himself, not discerning the Lord's body.* (1 Corinthians 11:23-29)

The Bible makes it clear that all who will follow Christ should observe this New Testament Passover in remembrance of His love and sacrifice for our sins and as a reminder of our commitment to Him for what God has done in our lives.

## Our Need to Observe the Feasts

According to 1 Corinthians 5:7-8, *"For even Christ our passover is sacrificed for us: Therefore let us keep the feast."*

Luke 22:19 gives specific instructions from the Savior: *"And he took bread, and gave thanks, and brake it, and gave unto them, saying, This is my body which is given for you: this do in remembrance of me."*

Now, as always, we have to first understand who are the children of Israel today? Granted, there is controversy on this subject, but most Bible scholars agree that Christians have been eternally blessed by being grafted into the family of God by faith in our Savior. Jesus even uses that picture-perfect example: *"I am the vine, ye are the branches: He that abideth in me, and I in him, the same bringeth forth much fruit: for without me ye can do nothing"* (John 15:5).

One of the most remarkable treasure lodes in all of Scripture is the study of the feasts which God outlined through the instructions He gave to Moses. Granted, some will say, "That's the Old Covenant. We live under the New Covenant since the death, burial, and resurrection of Jesus Christ took place. It is true; we do live under the New Covenant that was provided through the Savior's passion and provision as the substitute for all our sins. We no longer have to offer blood sacrifices and hold fast to a rigid set of rituals. According to Hebrews 10:1-10 (GW):

> *Moses's Teachings with their yearly cycle of sacrifices are only a shadow of the good things in the future. They aren't an exact likeness of those things. They can never make those who worship perfect. If these sacrifices could have made the worshipers perfect, the sacrifices would have stopped long ago. Those who worship would have been cleansed once and for all. Their consciences would have been free from sin. Instead, this yearly cycle of sacrifices reminded people of their sins. (The blood of bulls and goats cannot take away sins.) For this reason, when Christ*

came into the world, he said, "You did not want sacrifices and offerings, but you prepared a body for me. You did not approve of burnt offerings and sacrifices for sin."

Then I said, "I have come! (It is written about me in the scroll of the book.) I have come to do what you want, my God." In this passage Christ first said, "You did not want sacrifices, offerings, burnt offerings, and sacrifices for sin. You did not approve of them." (These are the sacrifices that Moses's Teachings require people to offer.) Then Christ says, "I have come to do what you want." He did away with sacrifices in order to establish the obedience that God wants. We have been set apart as holy because Jesus Christ did what God wanted him to do by sacrificing his body once and for all.

Jesus offered Himself as a sacrifice for our sins, "once and for all," so we don't have to live under the curse of the law. We are free to serve Him under the New Covenant. However, you cannot fully understand the New Covenant until you grasp the meaning of the Old Covenant. Neither can you truly appreciate all Jesus did for each of us on the cross until you peer closely into the meaning of the feasts of Israel, especially the Passover.

These principles are for all the feasts, which were given not just to the children of Israel but to Christians today who have been grafted into God's family through the Savior's sacrifice. We should study and observe these feasts, asking the Father for wisdom in understanding the truths in each feast. There is such a wealth of information to study. Our lives can be revolutionized through these feasts. The secret to seeing God's truth at work in your life comes through having spiritual eyes and obedience to the wisdom that He imparts to you as He seeks to impact your life forever!

# CHAPTER 3

# SEVEN BLESSINGS UNLEASHED IN YOUR LIFE

✌

Seven is a very important number in the Bible. It means perfection, completion, and salvation. After the six days of creation, God rested on the seventh day, not because he was tired, of course; here the word *rest* means "completion and satisfaction."

There are many more sevens. *Dake's Annotated Reference Bible* offers these lists: 435 groups of "seven," six "sevenfolds," two "sevens," 119 collections of "seventh," and 61 sets of "seventy." By itself, that is enough study material for a lifetime, so I won't belabor the point. Let me offer just a few examples of notable sevens:

- To allow the ground to rest and replenish, the nation of Israel was commanded in Leviticus 25:1-7 to refrain from farming the land every seven years.

- In addition to the "year of release" every seven years and after seven "Sabbaths of the land" (forty-nine years), the next year (the fiftieth) was the Jubilee year in which all slaves were freed and all debts released (Leviticus 25:8-13).

- Daniel 9 points to the ten clusters of seven weeks which were "determined" on the Hebrews, during which God sought to bring redemption, perfection, and completion in His chosen people: *"Seventy weeks are determined upon thy people and upon thy holy city, to finish the transgression, and to make an end of sins, and to make reconciliation for iniquity, and to bring in everlasting righteousness, and to seal up the vision and prophecy, and to anoint the most Holy"* (9:24).

- God has allocated man a symbolic prophetic week—*"One day is with the Lord as a thousand years"* (2 Peter 3:8)—during which mankind has six "days" to "work out his own salvation." According to Revelation 20, the six thousand years will be followed by the Millennium (the word *millennium* is not in the Bible, but it comes from the two Latin words *mille*, meaning "a thousand," and *annus*, meaning "years"). The purpose of the Millennium is to restore the Father's original divine order and plan: *"Blessed and holy is he that hath part in the first resurrection: on such the second death hath no power, but they shall be priests of God and of Christ, and shall reign with him a thousand years"* (Revelation 20:6).

- The book of Revelation outlines the completion of this age and uses the number seven more than fifty times (including seven angels, seven vials, seven seals, seven trumpets, and seven bowls).

Seven is obviously very important to God. So it is with the seven feasts of the Lord. These seven "appointed times" were given for a specific purpose so He could meet with mankind for His holy purposes.

## Seven Blessings

Let's look back at Exodus 23, a very revealing passage of Scripture and one that Christians have ignored for too long. It focuses on the feasts of the Passover season, and in this passage are seven specific blessings of the Passover (all references NKJV):

1. God will assign an angel to you: *"Behold, I send an Angel before you to keep you in the way and to bring you into the place which I have prepared"* (verse 20); and *"For My Angel will go before you"* (verse 23).

2. God will be an enemy to your enemies: *"But if you indeed obey His voice and do all that I speak, then I will be an enemy to your enemies and an adversary to your adversaries"* (verse 22).

3. God will give you prosperity: *"So you shall serve the LORD your God, and He will bless your bread and your water"* (verse 25).

4. God will take sickness away from you: *"And I will take sickness away from the midst of you"* (verse 25).

5. God will give you a long life: *"No one shall suffer miscarriage or be barren in your land; I will fulfill the number of your days"* (verse 26).

6. God will bring increase and inheritance: *"Little by little I will drive them out from before you, until you have increased, and you inherit the land"* (verse 30).

7. God will give a special year of blessing: *"And I will set your bounds from the Red Sea to the sea, Philistia, and from the desert to the River. For I will deliver the inhabitants of the land into your hand, and you shall drive them out before you"* (verse 31); and what the enemy stole will be returned to you and protected by God from being overtaken: *"I will not drive them out from before you in one year, lest the land become desolate and the beast of the field become too numerous for you"* (verse 29).

These Passover season blessings are very specific and astounding, which is why I spend an entire chapter on each blessing throughout part 2 of the book.

## Your Blessings Unleashed

When God offers a covenant with His people, as He does with the seven blessings of the Passover, it is a mutual obligation. Notice in the Exodus 23 passage, there is a prerequisite to all these blessings found in verse 15 as the children of Israel were given instructions for the Passover season: *"None shall appear before me empty."*

Granted, the children of Israel were required to bring more than twenty different offerings to the Lord, both great and small. During the Passover season, however, the offering was unique by resulting in seven specific blessings.

During the first season of the Jewish year—the Feasts of Passover, Unleavened Bread, and Firstfruits—God commanded the entire nation of Israel to honor Him by brining the first crops of their harvest to the house of the Lord. The Hebrews were forbidden to use even the smallest part of the harvest until an offering was made of the harvest's firstfruits. Giving these firstfruit Passover season offerings was considered a pure act of obedience to God, who is the Giver of all good things.

We shouldn't confuse this offering with the tithe of 10 percent of our income. That, technically, is not an offering because it belongs exclusively to the Lord. When we bring our tithe to the Lord we really don't give Him anything. Of course, we are blessed by the Lord for bringing our tithe as Malachi 3:7-12 affirms:

> *Even from the days of your fathers ye are gone away from mine ordinances, and have not kept them. Return unto me, and I will return unto you, saith the LORD of hosts. But ye said, Wherein shall we return? Will a man rob God? Yet ye have robbed me. But ye say, Wherein have we robbed thee? In tithes and offerings. Ye are cursed with a curse: for ye have robbed me, even this whole nation. Bring ye all the tithes into the storehouse, that there may be meat in mine house, and prove me now herewith, saith the LORD of hosts, if I will not open you the windows of heaven, and pour you out a blessing, that there shall not be room enough to receive it.*
>
> *And I will rebuke the devourer for your sakes, and he shall not destroy the fruits of your ground; neither shall your vine cast*

*her fruit before the time in the field, saith the LORD of hosts. And all nations shall call you blessed: for ye shall be a delightsome land, saith the LORD of hosts.*

We can no longer afford to rob God of either the tithes or offerings. The tithe, after all, opens "the windows of heaven." The Passover offering moves far beyond the blessings of the tithes into the "not be room enough to receive it" realm of supernatural increase.

The Word of God is filled with references to Passover and firstfruit blessings, but one of the most obvious is found in Proverbs 3:9-10 (NKJV):

*Honor the LORD with your possessions,*
*And with the firstfruits of all your increase;*
*So your barns will be filled with plenty,*
*And your vats will overflow with new wine.*

Would you like that kind of a life?

## The Passover Offering

The Passover and other holy days were so important that God told us to observe them forever (Exodus 12:14; Leviticus 23:14). He commanded us, as we observe these holy days, not to stand before Him empty-handed (Exodus 23:15).

We know that God instituted Passover when Israel left Egypt to go to the Promised Land. Every family purchased a lamb, which was their offering. They killed the lamb and put the blood of that lamb on the door post as God had commanded. Money was given in exchange for the lamb and protection. Then God said made it clear that believers should never forget this holy day called the Passover.

Deuteronomy 16:16-17 echoes other verses throughout the Scripture: *"And they shall not appear before the LORD empty-handed.*

*Every man shall give as he is able, according to the blessing of the* LORD *your God which He has given you"* (NKJV).

Amazing things happen when obedient people unleash God's supernatural blessings through the Passover season offering! The Passover offering reminds us of what God has done for us. We must bring our firstfruits to God with great thanksgiving.

What are your firstfruits? What Passover offering should you bring? First of all, we know that it is an offering during the Passover season, but it is not our tithe. In Bible times it was the first lamb from each mother sheep. Today, it can be the first paycheck from a new job or a portion of each new paycheck that you receive. It can be a portion from the sale of real estate property. It can be whatever God supplies. It should be sacrificial. It reflects your trust and faith in a God of abundance.

And the most exciting part is that each of the seven blessings of Passover has a powerful influence on those around you. What do I mean?

## Seven Blessings for Your Entire Household

Exodus 12:3-4 points to an amazing principle foretold during the Passover then fulfilled through Jesus Christ:

> *Speak ye unto all the congregation of Israel, saying, In the tenth day of this month they shall take to them every man a lamb, according to the house of their fathers, a lamb for an house: And if the household be too little for the lamb, let him and his neighbour next unto his house take it according to the number of the souls; every man according to his eating shall make your count for the lamb.*

God's intention, from the first Passover, was a lamb sacrificed for each house. It wasn't a lamb for each person. The shed blood was to cover every person in the household. It wasn't just the father, but fathers. It wasn't just the mother, but mothers. The protection included uncles, aunts, and cousins. And if you will look again at verse 4, the neighbors could even be protected by the shed blood of the lamb.

Certainly, every person in the household had the free choice of whether to stay in the house which was protected by the blood, just as each individual in a house has free will to decide whether to accept Jesus Christ as Savior, just as each person has the choice whether to receive the seven Passover offering blessings. However, it is God's desire to protect and bless the entire household. And this principle didn't start with the Passover. Even back in Genesis 7:1, the Bible declares, *"And the LORD said unto Noah, Come thou and all thy house into the ark; for thee have I seen righteous before me in this generation."*

In Joshua 24:15, we read:

> *And if it seem evil unto you to serve the LORD, choose you this day whom ye will serve; whether the gods which your fathers served that were on the other side of the flood, or the gods of the Amorites, in whose land ye dwell: but as for me and my house, we will serve the LORD.*

Fast-forward to the New Testament. Acts 16:14-15 shares the story of the Lydia, a new believer in Jesus:

> *A seller of purple, of the city of Thyatira, which worshiped God, heard us: whose heart the Lord opened, that she attended unto the things which were spoken of Paul. And when she was baptized, and her household, she besought us, saying, If ye have judged me to be faithful to the Lord, come into my house, and abide there. And she constrained us.*

Recorded later in that same chapter, the Philippian jailer became not only a new believer but also witnessed the miracle of household salvation:

*Sirs, what must I do to be saved? And they said, Believe on the Lord Jesus Christ, and thou shalt be saved, and thy house. And they spake unto him the word of the Lord, and to all that were in his house. And he took them the same hour of the night, and washed their stripes; and was baptized, he and all his, straightway. And when he had brought them into his house, he set meat before them, and rejoiced, believing in God with all his house.* (Acts 16:30-34)

Acts 18:8 shares a similar account: *"And Crispus, the chief ruler of the synagogue, believed on the Lord with all his house; and many of the Corinthians hearing believed, and were baptized."*

Because of the principle of a lamb for a house, you have the legal right to claim every member of your family for Christ. You have the same right to claim salvation for your neighbors. You also have the honor of claiming the seven blessings of Passover.

The promise is yours. There is an umbrella of grace over you and your household. You can build a powerful "more than enough" heritage, starting with your loved ones.

The secret of all the Passover season blessings, revealed individually in the next seven chapters, is very clear-cut: *"And they shall not appear before the LORD empty-handed"* (Deuteronomy 16:16, NKJV).

Come with your Passover offering. Prove God. Then watch Him pour out more blessings than you can hold (which means you will have to share with others, but we'll discuss more about that in chapter 12).

Amazing things are just ahead! Are you ready?

# PART TWO

# The Seven Passover Blessings

# CHAPTER 4

# BLESSING 1:
# GOD WILL ASSIGN
# AN ANGEL TO YOU

A S THE VERY FIRST OF SEVEN Passover blessings, God gave this amazing promise: *"Behold, I send an Angel before you to keep you in the way and to bring you into the place which I have prepared.... For My Angel will go before you"* (Exodus 23:20, 23, NKJV).

As you observe the Passover by bringing your firstfruit offering, an angel of God is assigned to keep you and lead you through your miracle-filled life. The Bible is filled with powerful examples:

- **First Passover**— After the first Passover, as the Israelites moved toward the Red Sea and prepared to leave Egypt, an angel was assigned to them ("went before them"), was visible in a pillar of cloud by day and a pillar of fire by night (Exodus 13:22), then went behind the multitude, protecting the children of Israel from the advancing Egyptian army (14:19-20).

- **Joshua**—As recorded in Joshua 5:11-15, after Moses died and Joshua became the leader of the Israelites, he commanded that they commemorate the Passover while they were in the plains of Jericho. In Jericho, Joshua looked up and saw a man holding a drawn sword. Joshua wanted to know who this person was there for: the Israelites or their enemies. The Bible calls this man "the captain of the host of the Lord." An amazing campaign of military victories followed as the children of Israel occupied their Promised Land.

🌿 **Gideon**—God called Gideon during the time of the Passover to save Israel from the hateful Midianites, but he did not feel worthy to do such a valorous thing: *"And he said unto him, Oh my Lord, wherewith shall I save Israel? behold, my family is poor in Manasseh, and I am the least in my father's house"* (Judges 6:15). Gideon then asked the Lord to remain in place there until he could bring a Passover offering. Then Gideon prepared the Passover meal and presented it to the Lord. After he gave the offering, it became more apparent than ever that a powerful angel was assigned to him. Gideon became a mighty leader, a wealthy man, and a supreme warrior for the cause of God, winning major battles against the enemy.

🌿 **Hezekiah**—His father, the previous king, had abolished the observance of the Passover in his day, and Israel had fallen on hard times. When Hezekiah became king, he reestablished the Passover offering. At the time, he was thirty-nine years old and dying. His pastor, Isaiah, came to visit him and gave him the word that in three days he would die. Hezekiah turned his face to the wall and prayed. He said to God, "Do you remember how I walked before you in truth and with a perfect heart? Do you remember how I have done those things that are right?" At that, God told Isaiah to go back and tell the king that fifteen years would be added to his life. That night, an angel of the Lord went out to the camp of Sennacherib, the captain of the Assyrians, and killed 185,000 people. God healed Hezekiah, extended his life, and killed his enemies. Hezekiah became a very wealthy man in the next fifteen years. All of this is found in 2 Chronicles 30 and 2 Kings 20.

🌿 **David**—In 2 Samuel 24, David decided to take a census of the people. An angel of the Lord was killing the men of Israel, and

David wanted the killing to stop. He wanted to buy a threshing floor and there make an altar to worship God. The owner of the threshing floor offered to give him the place, but David refused: *"And the king said unto Araunah, Nay; but I will surely buy it of thee at a price: neither will I offer burnt offerings unto the LORD my God of that which doth cost me nothing. So David bought the threshingfloor and the oxen for fifty shekels of silver. And David built there an altar unto the LORD, and offered burnt offerings and peace offerings. So the LORD was intreated for the land, and the plague was stayed from Israel"* (verses 24-25).

❧ **Jesus**—Not only did the Savior observe the Passover with His disciples in the Upper Room, he then offered Himself as the perfect Passover Lamb. When He was in the garden, before His crucifixion, He was tempted to back out of dying for the sins of every person of Adam's race: *"And he was withdrawn from them about a stone's cast, and kneeled down, and prayed, Saying, Father, if thou be willing, remove this cup from me: nevertheless not my will, but thine, be done. And there appeared an angel unto him from heaven, strengthening him"* (Luke 22:41-43). The angel of the Lord came and helped ready Him for the task that was ahead, an unprecedented agony memorialized in Hebrews 12:2: *"Looking unto Jesus the author and finisher of our faith; who for the joy that was set before him endured the cross, despising the shame, and is set down at the right hand of the throne of God."*

❧ **Peter**—Acts 12 gives the awe-inspiring account of how Peter was in jail for preaching the gospel of Jesus Christ. It was Passover season. We know that Peter and the other disciples observed the feast. We also know that an "angel of the Lord" was dispatched to deliver the apostle from prison: *"And, behold, the angel of the Lord came upon him, and a light shined in the prison: and he smote Peter on the side, and raised him up, saying, Arise up quickly. And his chains fell off from his hands"* (verse 7).

❧ **Paul**—Acts 27 records how the apostle Paul was on board a storm-tossed ship for fourteen days and nights. It appeared that all on the vessel would be lost. He celebrated the Passover, and as he did, an angel of the Lord stood by him, encouraging him. The miracle survival that happened next on the raging waves is one for the ages.

# Angels

Since assigned angels are the first blessing of the Passover offering, it is important to know more about them. There are 158 references to angels in the Old Testament. In the New Testament there are 178. Angels are mentioned in almost every book of the Bible, and the first two chapters of the book of Hebrews tell us more about angels than any other passage in Scripture.

There are numerous examples how angels have been involved in the events of mankind. Let me offer a brief list with references for future study:

- They are numerous (Genesis 32:2).

- Angels are associated with visions of God (Exodus 3:2).

- Angels were created before humans (Job 38:7).

- There are different classifications of angels (Psalm 80:1; Isaiah 6:2).

- Satan was created as a beautiful angel of light who rebelled against God (Isaiah 14:12; Luke 10:18).

- Angels are spiritual beings (Matthew 22:30).

- The angels worshiped when Jesus came into the world (Luke 2:13; Hebrews 1:6).

- Angels are joyful about and fascinated by the salvation that God provided for a fallen human race (Luke 15:10; 1 Peter 1:12).

- Believers are urged to be hospitable, for some have entertained angels without even realizing it (Hebrews 13:2).

This list includes some of the most notable appearances of God's messengers:

- God's angels protected Lot (Genesis 19).

- God's angels delivered Hagar and Ishmael (Genesis 21).

- Angels guided Abraham's servant (Genesis 24:7).

- God's angel protected Jacob from Laban (Genesis 31).

- God protected Jacob all his life (Genesis 48:16).

- The angel who "went before" the Israelites during the Exodus and protected them from the Egyptian army, also guided God's chosen people on their journey after crossing the Red Sea. Each day the angel, visible in the cloudy and fiery pillars, showed the way God wanted them to go (Numbers 14:14), even during the wilderness journey (Nehemiah 9:12).

- God's angel protected Israel from an Egyptian army (Exodus 14:19).

- Angels guided Israel throughout the Exodus (Exodus 23:20; 32:34; Judges 2:1).

- God's angel brought Israel from slavery to the edge of the Promised Land (Numbers 20:16).

- God's angel brought Israel to the Promised Land (Judges 2:1)

- God's angel guided the parents of Samson (Judges 13:8–9).

- God's angel guided Elijah (2 Kings 1:15).

- God's angel protected Jerusalem from an invading army (2 Kings 19:35).

- An angel protected Shadrach, Meshach, and Abed-nego from death in a fiery furnace (Daniel 3).

- An angel protected Daniel from hungry lions (Daniel 6).

- An angel guided Joseph to wed Mary (Matthew 1:20).

- An angel protected Jesus from Herod's plot, advising Joseph when to leave Bethlehem and when to go to Nazareth (Matthew 2).

- Angels could have protected Jesus from those who crucified Him (Matthew 26:53).

- God's angel delivered the apostles from prison (Acts 5).

- An angel guided Philip to Gaza (Acts 8:26).

- God's angel guided Cornelius to send for Peter (Acts 10:3; 11:13).

- God's angel delivered Peter from Agrippa (Acts 12).

Today, perhaps, we perceive these to be heavenly messengers or representatives (both are definitions for the Hebrew word for angel, *mal'ak*). Hebrews 1:14 refers to angels with this question: *"Are they not all ministering spirits, sent forth to minister for them who shall be heirs of salvation?"*

Lester Sumrall, in his book *Angels: The Messengers of God* writes: "It is the obligation and privilege of modern Christians to understand and use the ministry of angels."[1]

John Calvin wrote:

The point on which the Scriptures specially insist is that which tends to our most comfort, and to the confirmation of our faith, namely, that angels are ministers and dispensers of the divine bounty toward us. Accordingly, we are told how they watch for our safety, how they undertake our defense, direct our path, and take heed that no evil befall us. There are whole passages which relate, in the first instance, to Christ, the Head of the Church, and after Him to all believers. "He shall give his angels charge over thee, to keep thee in all thy ways. And they shall bear thee up in their hands, lest thou dash thy foot against a stone." Again, "The angel of the Lord encampeth round about them that fear him, and delivereth them." By these passages the Lord shows that the protection of those whom he had undertaken to defend he has delegated to his angels.[2]

Dr. Billy Graham lifted the veil between the visible and the invisible world to give us an eye-opening account of these behind-the-scenes agents in his 1975 best-selling book about angels. In it are the experiences of Dr. Graham and others who are convinced that at moments of special need they have been attended by God's messengers. Dr. Graham wrote:

> The angels are observing firsthand the building of the body of the true Church in all places of his dominion at this very hour.... But what are they thinking as we live in the world's arena? Do they observe us as we stand fast in the faith and walk in righteousness? Or may they be wondering at our lack of commitment? Our certainty that angels right now witness how we are walking through life should mightily influence the decisions we make. God is watching, and His angels are interested spectators, too.[3]

## Blessings of an Angel Assigned to You

Studies of angels have filled volumes. Anyone who begins a study cannot help but be surprised at how many wonderful blessings an angel can bring. Let's take a quick tour through the Word of God. Although certainly not exhaustive, here are some of blessings that can happen when an angel is assigned to you.

**Angels cause us to prosper on our way**—"*And he said unto me, The LORD, before whom I walk, will send his angel with thee, and prosper* *thy way; and thou shalt take a wife for my son of my kindred, and of my father's house"* (Genesis 24:40).

**Angels protect and guide us**—*"For mine Angel shall go before thee, and bring thee in unto the Amorites, and the Hittites, and the Perizzites, and the Canaanites, and the Hivites, and the Jebusites: and I will cut them off"* (Exodus 23:23).

**Angels persist until their assignments are finished**—*"Then the LORD opened the eyes of Balaam, and he saw the angel of the LORD standing in the way, and his sword drawn in his hand: and he bowed down his head, and fell flat on his face. And the angel of the LORD said unto him, Wherefore hast thou smitten thine ass these three times? behold, I went out to withstand thee"* (Numbers 22:31-32).

**Angels can be God's agents of wrath against the enemy**—*"And it came to pass, when Joshua was by Jericho, that he lifted up his eyes and looked, and, behold, there stood a man over against him with his sword drawn in his hand: and Joshua went unto him, and said unto him, Art thou for us, or for our adversaries? And he said, Nay; but as captain of the host of the LORD am I now come. And Joshua fell on his face to the earth, and did worship, and said unto him, What saith my lord unto his servant?"* (Joshua 5:13-14).

**Angels bring peace and increase the faith of believers**—*"And the angel of the LORD appeared unto him, and said unto him, The LORD is with thee, thou mighty man of valour.... And when Gideon perceived that he was an angel of the LORD, Gideon said, Alas, O LORD! for because I have seen an angel of the LORD face to face. And the LORD said unto him, Peace be unto thee; fear not: thou shalt not die"* (Judges 6:12, 22-23).

**Angels can be agents of God's encouragement**—*"And the angel of the LORD appeared unto him, and said unto him, The LORD is with thee, thou mighty man of valour"* (Judges 6:12).

**Angels can be God's agents of war**—*"And when the servant of the man of God was risen early, and gone forth, behold, an host compassed the city both with horses and chariots. And his servant said unto him, Alas,* *my master! how shall we do? And he answered, Fear not: for they that be with us are more than they that be with them. And Elisha prayed, and said, LORD, I pray thee, open his eyes, that he may see. And the LORD opened the eyes of the young man; and he saw: and, behold, the mountain was full of horses and chariots of fire round about Elisha"* (2 Kings 6:15-17).

**Angels surround us and deliver us**— *"The angel of the LORD encampeth round about them that fear him, and delivereth them"* (Psalm 34:7).

**God gives angels charge over us**— *"For he shall give his angels charge over thee, to keep thee in all thy ways. They shall bear thee up in their hands, lest thou dash thy foot against a stone"* (Psalm 91:11-12).

**Angels hear God's voice and obey His commands**— *"Bless the LORD, ye his angels, that excel in strength, that do his commandments, hearkening unto the voice of his word"* (Psalm 103:20).

**Angels are God's ministers who do the Father's pleasure**— *"Bless ye the LORD, all ye his hosts; ye ministers of his, that do his pleasure"* (Psalm 103:21).

**Angels praise God**— *"Praise ye him, all his angels: praise ye him, all his hosts"* (Psalm 148:2).

**Angels guard the throne of God**— *"In the year that king Uzziah died I saw also the Lord sitting upon a throne, high and lifted up, and his train filled the temple. Above it stood the seraphims: each one had six wings; with twain he covered his face, and with twain he covered his feet, and with twain he did fly"* (Isaiah 6:1-2).

**Angels can be defending warriors**— *"By the way that he came, by the same shall he return, and shall not come into this city, saith the LORD. For I will defend this city to save it for mine own sake, and for my servant David's sake. Then the angel of the LORD went forth, and smote in the camp of the Assyrians a hundred and fourscore and five thousand: and when they arose early in the morning, behold, they were all dead corpses"* (Isaiah 37:34-36).

**Angels keep watch over believers**— *"I saw in the visions of my head upon my bed, and, behold, a watcher and an holy one came down from heaven"* (Daniel 4:13).

**Angels can be God's agents of protection**—*"My God hath sent his angel, and hath shut the lions' mouths, that they have not hurt me: forasmuch as before him innocency was found in me; and also before thee, O king, have I done no hurt"* (Daniel 6:22).

**Angels bring messages from God**—*"And it came to pass, when I, even I Daniel, had seen the vision, and sought for the meaning, then, behold, there stood before me as the appearance of a man. And I heard a man's voice between the banks of Ulai, which called, and said, Gabriel, make this man to understand the vision"* (Daniel 8:15-16).

**Angels can be sent to answer prayers**—*"Yea, whiles I was speaking in prayer, even the man Gabriel, whom I had seen in the vision at the beginning, being caused to fly swiftly, touched me about the time of the evening oblation. And he informed me, and talked with me, and said, O Daniel, I am now come forth to give thee skill and understanding. At the beginning of thy supplications the commandment came forth, and I am come to shew thee; for thou art greatly beloved: therefore understand the matter, and consider the vision"* (Daniel 9:21-23).

**Angels remind God's people of the Father's love**—*"And, behold, an hand touched me, which set me upon my knees and upon the palms of my hands. And he said unto me, O Daniel, a man greatly beloved, understand the words that I speak unto thee, and stand upright: for unto thee am I now sent. And when he had spoken this word unto me, I stood trembling"* (Daniel 10:10-11).

**Angels minister peace and encouragement**—*"Then said he unto me, Fear not, Daniel: for from the first day that thou didst set thine heart to understand, and to chasten thyself before thy God, thy words were heard, and I am come for thy words"* (Daniel 10:12).

**Angels can be God's agents of warning**—*"And when they were departed, behold, the angel of the Lord appeareth to Joseph in a dream, saying, Arise, and take the young child and his mother, and flee into Egypt, and be thou there until I bring thee word: for Herod will seek the young child to destroy him"* (Matthew 2:13).

**Angels will help reap the end-time harvest**—*"The enemy that sowed them is the devil; the harvest is the end of the world; and the reapers are the angels"* (Matthew 13:39).

**Angels minister to children**—*"Take heed that ye despise not one of these little ones; for I say unto you, That in heaven their angels do always behold the face of my Father which is in heaven"* (Matthew 18:10).

**Angels are God's agents of instruction and guidance**—*"But the angel said unto him, Fear not, Zacharias: for thy prayer is heard; and thy wife Elisabeth shall bear thee a son, and thou shalt call his name John"* (Luke 1:13).

**Angels rejoice when a person is saved**—*"Likewise, I say unto you, there is joy in the presence of the angels of God over one sinner that repenteth"* (Luke 15:10).

**Angels strengthen believers**—*"And there appeared an angel unto him from heaven, strengthening him"* (Luke 22:43).

**Angels communicate God's instructions**—*"And the angel of the Lord spake unto Philip, saying, Arise, and go toward the south unto the way that goeth down from Jerusalem unto Gaza, which is desert"* (Acts 8:26).

**Angels minister specifically to believers**—*"And of the angels he saith, Who maketh his angels spirits, and his ministers a flame of fire. . . . But to which of the angels said he at any time, Sit on my right hand, until I make thine enemies thy footstool? Are they not all ministering spirits, sent forth to minister for them who shall be heirs of salvation?"* (Hebrews 1:7, 13-14).

**Angels are ever vigilant**—*"And the four beasts had each of them six wings about him; and they were full of eyes within: and they rest not day and night, saying, Holy, holy, holy, Lord God Almighty, which was, and is, and is to come"* (Revelation 4:8).

**Angels surround God's throne**—*"And I beheld, and I heard the voice of many angels round about the throne and the beasts and the elders:*

*and the number of them was ten thousand times ten thousand, and thousands of thousands; Saying with a loud voice, Worthy is the Lamb that was slain to receive power, and riches, and wisdom, and strength, and honour, and glory, and blessing"* (Revelation 5:11-12).

**Angels worship God**—*"And all the angels stood round about the throne, and about the elders and the four beasts, and fell before the throne on their faces, and worshipped God, Saying, Amen: Blessing, and glory, and wisdom, and thanksgiving, and honour, and power, and might, be unto our God for ever and ever. Amen"* (Revelation 7:11-12).

**Angels present the prayers of the saints before God's throne**—*"And another angel came and stood at the altar, having a golden censer; and there was given unto him much incense, that he should offer it with the prayers of all saints upon the golden altar which was before the throne. And the smoke of the incense, which came with the prayers of the saints, ascended up before God out of the angel's hand"* (Revelation 8:3-4).

**Angels war against the enemy and win battles**—*"And there was war in heaven: Michael and his angels fought against the dragon; and the dragon fought and his angels, And prevailed not; neither was their place found any more in heaven"* (Revelation 12:7-8).

**Angels guard the holy gates**—*"And he carried me away in the spirit to a great and high mountain, and shewed me that great city, the holy Jerusalem, descending out of heaven from God, Having the glory of God: and her light was like unto a stone most precious, even like a jasper stone, clear as crystal; And had a wall great and high, and had twelve gates, and at the gates twelve angels, and names written thereon, which are the names of the twelve tribes of the children of Israel"* (Revelation 21:10-12).

**Angels can be God's agents of revelation**—*"And I John saw these things, and heard them. And when I had heard and seen, I fell down to worship before the feet of the angel which shewed me these things"* (Revelation 22:8).

**Angels are servants**—*"Then saith he unto me, See thou do it not: for I am thy fellowservant, and of thy brethren the prophets, and of them which keep the sayings of this book: worship God"* (Revelation 22:9).

Of the more than three hundred references to angels from Genesis to Revelation, more than a third of them are seen talking to people, giving direction, and teaching how to live before God.

Do angels still intervene in the lives of believers? Dr. Billy Graham writes these thought-provoking words:

> Angels belong to a uniquely different dimension of creation that we, limited to the natural order, can scarcely comprehend.... [God] has given angels higher knowledge, power and mobility than we.... They are God's messengers whose chief business is to carry out His orders in the world. He has given them an ambassadorial charge. He has designated and empowered them as holy deputies.[4]

Gladys Aylward, a well-known English missionary to China, stayed to help Chinese children long after the Communists had taken over mainland China. She has told story after story of God sending angels to protect her and those precious Chinese children.

The late Pastor Richard Wurmbrand, author of *Tortured for Christ* and one of Romania's most widely known leaders, pastors, and educators, was an evangelical minister who withstood fourteen years of Communist imprisonment and torture. In 1945 when the Communists seized Romania and attempted to control the churches for their purposes, Richard Wurmbrand immediately began an effective "underground" ministry for his enslaved people and the invading Russian soldiers. He was eventually arrested in 1948 and spent three years in solitary confinement. He later told of the angels that ministered to him while he was in solitary confinement in a Communist prison in Romania.

Corrie ten Boom, in her book *Marching Orders for the End Battle*, described an experience in the Congo during a particularly dangerous insurgency:

> When the rebels advanced on a school where two hundred children of missionaries lived, they planned to kill both the children and teachers. Those in the school knew of the danger and therefore went to prayer. Their only protection was a fence and a couple of soldiers, while the enemy, who came closer and closer, amounted to several hundred.
>
> When the rebels were close by, suddenly something happened: they turned around and ran away! The next day the same thing happened, and again on the third day.
>
> One of the rebels was wounded and was brought to the mission hospital. While the doctor was busy dressing his wounds, he asked him: "Why did you not break into the school as you planned?"
>
> "We could not do it. We saw hundreds of soldiers in white uniforms and we became scared."
>
> In Africa soldiers never wear white uniforms, so it must have been angels. What a wonderful thing that the Lord can open the eyes of the enemy so that they see angels! We, as children of God, do not need to see them with our human eyes. We have the Bible and faith, and by faith we see invisible things.

Yes, God still intervenes in the lives of believers! Now, more than ever, the blessing of assigned angels is relevant to believers. Their appearances are not relegated to the Old or New Testaments. In fact, the *New Unger's Bible Dictionary* notes: "Angels appear most frequently and conspicuously in connection with the coming and ministry of our Lord."[5] Believe it or not, angels are mentioned more in the book of Revelation than in other book in the Bible.

Best of all, quoting Lester Sumrall, we will spend eternity with the angels: "[Angels] were not made for a brief period of time. Throughout eternity we will have fellowship with the angels of god, just like we have fellowship with the redeemed who have been living for Jesus during all these year."[6]

## The Blessing

I've been told that a Google Internet word search for *angels* brings up a list of more than a half-million entries. Obviously, people want to know about angels. Much of the information that is available is hardly based on Scripture.

The reason I have offered numerous Bible references is specifically for that reason. As you are assigned your angel as a result of the Passover blessing, it is vital that you understand that God's Word is the only source of truth about angels.

It is my prayer that God will bless you mightily as you learn more about His heavenly messengers, for they are powerful and important spiritual beings who so greatly affect our lives here on earth!

# CHAPTER 5

# BLESSING 2: GOD WILL BE AN ENEMY TO YOUR ENEMIES

ONCE YOU BEGIN TO OBSERVE the Passover, you can expect God to be an enemy to your enemies. He has promised to do so: *"But if you indeed obey His voice and do all that I speak, then I will be an enemy to your enemies and an adversary to your adversaries"* (Exodus 23:22, NKJV).

As with each of the seven blessings throughout this book, the Bible gives many examples of people who were blessed as a result of their observance of the Passover Feast:

- **Israelites**—In Exodus 14, after the children of Israel observed the Passover and exited Egypt, they quickly met a major roadblock in their path to freedom—the Red Sea. Can you imagine the scene? With Pharaoh's army on their heels, God became an enemy to the enemy. The sea was rolled back on either side to expose a dry riverbed that they could walk upon. The multitude, upward to 3 million Hebrews, hurried across this wonderful boulevard of escape. Just as the last Israelite got to the other side of the Red Sea, God released the waters, drowning their physical enemies, the Egyptian army.

✌ **Joshua**—Recorded in Joshua 6, after the "captain of the host of the Lord" appeared to Joshua, assuring him that God was on his side, the army of Israel, under Joshua's leadership, caused the walls of Jericho to fall down. The army of Israel took the city and went forward to their Promised Land.

✌ **Gideon**—Faced with a massive army, Gideon was locked in an all-or-nothing situation: *"And the Midianites and the Amalekites and all the children of the east lay along in the valley like grasshoppers for multitude; and their camels were without number, as the sand by the sea side for multitude"* (Judges 7:12). With his little band of three hundred men, he handily routed the enemy with one of the most unusual of all weapons: *"And he divided the three hundred men into three companies, and he put a trumpet in every man's hand, with empty pitchers, and lamps within the pitchers. . . . And the three hundred blew the trumpets, and the LORD set every man's sword against his fellow, even throughout all the host"* (Judges 7:16, 22). No one doubted the fact that God caused the miracle against Gideon's enemies.

✌ **Hezekiah**—God not only restored the life He had intended to take from Hezekiah, but He also defeated, using an angel, the Assyrians that were threatening the king and his country (2 Chronicles 32:20-22).

✌ **David**—King Saul, David's father-in-law, was trying to kill this God-appointed successor to his throne (1 Samuel 18:27-29). Time after time, God miraculously enabled David to escape Saul's clutches, and eventually brought about the dramatic end to Saul's life (1 Samuel 31). God was really an "enemy to his enemies" in David's case.

✌ **Peter**—In Acts 12, Peter was in jail because Herod hated those who were spreading the Gospel successfully. Herod had killed James the brother of John, and he wanted to kill Peter, also. However, God became an enemy to Peter's enemies and miraculously allowed him to walk free from the prison and Herod's clutches.

🐟 **Paul**—I have already mentioned the miracle on the raging waves. Over and over, Paul faced certain death as he traveled about the world telling the good news of Jesus's life, death, and resurrection. Once a deadly snake was his enemy, latching on to his flesh to pass the poison into Paul's body: *"And when the barbarians saw the venomous beast hang on his hand, they said among themselves, No doubt this man is a murderer, whom, though he hath escaped the sea, yet vengeance suffereth not to live. And he shook off the beast into the fire, and felt no harm. Howbeit they looked when he should have swollen, or fallen down dead suddenly: but after they had looked a great while, and saw no harm come to him, they changed their minds, and said that he was a god"* (Acts 28:4-6). I love the response of the people on Melita Island. Within moments, Paul went from being a horrible criminal, unfit to live, to being a "god." The true God was truly an enemy to Paul's enemies, and the miracle the islanders witnessed undoubtedly opened doors for ministry.

What a wonderful blessing to the observers of Passover! When things come against you, God intervenes and destroys your enemies!

## History

It is important to remember how God established the "enemy to your enemies" blessing. Remember when the Lord told Moses that the children of Israel would be spared from the death of the firstborn during the Passover? Each family was to follow these seven instructions found in Exodus 12:

1.  Choose a one-year-old male lamb or goat without blemish for the Passover offering (verse 5).

2.  Join together with small families that cannot use a whole lamb (verse 4).

3.  Keep the lamb for four days before slaughter (verse 6).

4.  Have the head of the household slay the lamb on the evening of the fourteenth day of the month (verse 6).

5.  Sprinkle the blood of the lamb on the sides and the tops of the door frames of the house (verse 7).

6.  Roast the lamb that evening and eat it with bitter herbs and unleavened bread (verse 8).

7.  Eat the meal in haste, with cloaks tucked into belts, sandals on feet, and staves in hands (verse 11).

God told them to prepare because He would pass over the land. *"For I will pass through the land of Egypt on that night, and will strike all the firstborn in the land of Egypt, both man and beast; and against all the gods of Egypt I will execute judgement: I am the Lord"* (verse 12).

Then the Lord gave this promise: *"Now the blood shall be a sign for you on the houses where you are. And when I see the blood, I will pass over you; and the plague whall not be on you to destroy you when I strike the land of Egypt"* (verse 13, NKJV).

At midnight on the night of the Passover, the firstborn in every Egyptian household died. The wailing was heard across the land even before the sun rose (verses 29-30). But in the houses of the Israelites there was not one dead. God was truly an enemy to the enemies of the children of Israel.

The first Passover was a shadow of what was to happen one day on a hill called Calvary. For at Calvary *"Christ, our Passover, was sacrificed for us"* (1 Corinthians 5:7, NKJV). There we were redeemed *"with the precious blood of Christ, as of a lamb without blemish and without spot"* (1 Peter 1:19). Our Savior gave His life as a sacrifice, once and for always, to destroy the enemy of the soul of every man, woman, and child who has ever lived.

## Your Authority as a Believer

Jesus offered amazing power to His followers, for He promised,

> *Behold, I give unto you power to tread on serpents and scorpions, and over all the power of the enemy: and nothing shall by any means hurt you. Notwithstanding in this rejoice not, that the spirits are subject unto you; but rather rejoice, because your names are written in heaven."* (Luke 10:19-20)

In his classic book *Guide to Spiritual Warfare*, the powerful Bible teacher E. M. Bounds referred to the phrase "over all the power of the enemy," putting the blessing in proper perspective:

> The Devil is the enemy of Christ and of man. Jesus gave His disciples power over all the Devil's power. To Christ the Devil was a very real person. He recognized his personality, felt and acknowledged his power, abhorred his character, and warred against his kingdom.[1]

Charles Spurgeon, considered one of the deepest Bible teachers of all time, wrote these words in his insightful book *Prayer and Spiritual Warfare*, speaking of the enemy of our souls:

> God comes in, takes up the quarrel personally, and causes him to be disgraced on the very battlefield upon which he had gained a temporary success. He tells the Dragon that He will undertake to deal with him; this quarrel would not be between the Serpent and man, but between God and the Serpent. God says, in solemn words, *"I will put enmity between thee and the woman, and between thy seed and her seed; it shall bruise thy head, and thou shalt bruise his heel"* (Genesis 3:15).... Let us always resist the Devil with this belief, that

he has received a broken head. I am inclined to think that Luther's way of laughing at the Devil was a good one, for he is worthy of shame and everlasting contempt. Luther once threw an inkstand at the Devil's head when he was tempting him very sorely. Though the act itself appears absurd enough, yet it was a true type of what that greater reformer was all his life long. The books he wrote were truly a flinging of the inkstand at the head of the Fiend.[2]

Remember this fact: God is not your enemy. God is for you. And as you discover this blessing of Passover, God becomes the enemy of your enemies. You can cry out with the psalmist, *"When I cry out to You, Then my enemies will turn back; This I know, because God is for me"* (Psalm 56:9, NKJV).

You can exclaim with Paul, *"What then shall we say to these things? If God is for us, who can be against us? He who did not spare His own Son, but delivered Him up for us all, how shall He not with Him also freely give us all things?"* (Romans 8:31-32, NKJV).

You can say with the writer of Hebrews, *"So we may boldly say: 'The LORD is my helper; I will not fear. What can man do to me?'"* (13:6, NKJV).

Throughout the centuries, there have been many enemies of God's people, but they are not the real enemy. They may be pawns of the real enemy. The devil is your enemy, and he is a vanquished foe.

## Protection for Your Household

As with the other Passover blessings, when God becomes an enemy to your enemies, your family is also offered a special protection.

As recorded in Exodus 12:3, why did the Lord tell the Israelites to find a lamb for the salvation of each household? The blessings of God's covenants can lead to salvation and protection for an entire family.

Remember what God said to Noah: *"Come thou and all thy house into the ark; for thee have I seen righteous before me in this generation"* (Genesis 7:1). The Passover blessing had not been proclaimed yet, but when this promise was given, Noah was the only pure and virtuous man the Lord could find, and because of His obedience, God told him that his entire household would find protection because of his actions.

In Genesis 19:29 we find that God delivered Lot out of Sodom because of His covenant with Abraham: *"God remembered Abraham, and sent Lot out of the midst of the overthrow"* (Genesis 19:29).

## Your Adversary

In the New Testament the sacrifice was made once and for all through Jesus Christ. So how do you stand upon this truth and claim the provision, protection, and deliverance that He has given us?

As the Word of Christ dwells richly in us, we become transformed. Faith is constructed of the Word and the Spirit, and faith is the body and substance of obedience to God's will. As you are obedient to the Passover offering, God has committed Himself, His purpose, and His promise to being the enemy of your enemies.

Now, let me give you a word of warning. Just when you think you have reached the top of any spiritual mountain, Satan will launch a major assault against you. If all good things come from the Father, then you know what comes from the evil one. The problems you face may be a marriage on the rocks, a child on drugs, or financial pressures that are unbearable. At times your mind can be invaded by troubling thoughts that just won't go away.

You can take the authority of God's Word. God is not looking simply for religious activity in your life. He desires that His power might flow through you. You are in combat with the forces of darkness. It is important to pray specifically for His power to flow through you:

*That the God of our Lord Jesus Christ, the Father of glory, may give unto you the spirit of wisdom and revelation in the knowledge of him: The eyes of your understanding being enlightened; that ye may know what is the hope of his calling, and what the riches of the glory of his inheritance in the saints, And what is the exceeding greatness of his power to us-ward who believe, according to the working of his mighty power.* (Ephesians 1:17-19)

What mighty power is available to us! As believers we are coheirs of God's rule and authority. We are *"heirs of God, and joint-heirs with Christ"* (Romans 8:17). His strength is ours through faith in Him.

Paul clearly declares that God has *"raised us up together, and made us sit together in the heavenly places in Christ Jesus"* (Ephesians 2:6). Today our position in Christ is settled. We don't have to beg for our "throne rights." As heirs of God and joint heirs with Christ, we only need to accept what is already ours. This power is magnified through the Passover blessing as our enemies become God Almighty's enemies. Psalm 56:9 declares, *"When I cry unto thee, then shall mine enemies turn back: this I know; for God is for me."* Because God if "for you," your enemies will be turned away!

## Winning the War

I have met many individuals who have allowed Satan to keep them in a perpetual state of worry and anxiety. They fail to comprehend that God is ready and able to fight their battles.

God said to the children of Israel after they observed Passover, *"I will give peace in the land, and ye shall lie down, and none shall make you afraid: and I will rid evil beasts out of the land, neither shall the sword go through your land. And ye shall chase your enemies, and they shall fall before you by the sword"* (Leviticus 26:6-7).

One of the great lessons in the Old Testament is that before you can be victorious in a physical battle, you must win the spiritual war. That war is won, in great part, through honoring Passover!

# CHAPTER 6

# BLESSING 3: GOD WILL GIVE YOU PROSPERITY

A s YOU ARE OBEDIENT TO GOD with your Passover offering, the Father has promised extraordinary prosperity: "*Ye shall serve the LORD your God, and he shall bless thy bread, and thy water*" (Exodus 23:25).

Using very simple terms, God taught how His blessing will make even basic staples as bread and water more refreshing and nourishing than a feast of lavish food and drink. In truth, once the children of Israel left the wilderness and entered their Promised Land, exaggerated prosperity was theirs. The scouts that had visited the land before the Israelites entered saw a land that produced an abundance of food for both man and beast.

This supernatural prosperity followed numerous examples of the Passover blessing of prosperity. Here are three quick studies:

* **David**—We know he was faithful in observing the Passover. We also know, from 1 Samuel 22, that he helped engineer one of the most amazing military and social transformations in recorded history. David, though already anointed by the prophet Samuel to be the next king of Israel, had to flee from the jealous King Saul. He was soon joined by an unlikely and

unsavory band of about four hundred followers: *"And every one that was in distress, and every one that was in debt, and every one that was discontented, gathered themselves unto him"* (22:2). As captain, what did he do? From his Holy Spirit–inspired notebook (the Psalms), we know that he began preaching victory and godly prosperity. The very first sentence in Psalm 1 begins with the word "blessed" (verse 1) followed closely with "like a tree planted by the rivers…that bringeth forth his fruit" and "prosper" (verse 3).

In the Twenty-third Psalm as he recognized God as his source for everything, he wrote these memorable words, *"The LORD is my shepherd, I shall not want"* (verse 1). In that same psalm, he declared, *"Surely goodness and mercy shall follow me all the days of my life: and I will dwell in the house of the LORD for ever"* (verse 6). In the Hebrew, the word for "goodness" is tied to the same root word as "plenteous in goods."

In Psalm 118:5, David acknowledged his negative circumstances, testifying of his God: *"I called upon the LORD, in distress: the LORD answered me, and set me in a large place."* In Hebrew this indicates a place of prosperity.

We are safe in assuming that David began preaching his message of prosperity and victory to his little band of formerly distressed, debt-ridden, and discontented followers. The results? Within one generation, the country was literally overrun with abundance. According to 2 Chronicles 1:15, by the time Solomon became king of Israel, silver and gold were as plenteous as stones. Can you imagine? David built a heritage and nation so prosperous that precious metals were as common as common rocks!

🕊 **Gideon**—In Judges 6:15 Gideon told God that he was the poorest in his tribe of Manasseh. Then, after the visit from the angel, and after Gideon led the march to defeat the Midianites, God caused great increase to come to him. (Judges 6—8:26)

🌿 Hezekiah—During this king of Israel's extended lifetime, the Bible records in 2 Kings 18—20 that the people had to build many more silos to accommodate the fabulous harvests they made. This would be equivalent in today's world of filling banks with personal wealth. Later, when his son Manasseh took the throne and no longer observed the Passover, all the wealth obtained by good Hezekiah was lost.

Then, as now, God offers the promise of prosperity to those who are obedient: *"But thou shalt remember the LORD thy God: for it is he that giveth thee power to get wealth, that he may establish his covenant which he sware unto thy fathers, as it is this day"* (Deuteronomy 8:18).

Though God promises abundance, let me hasten to say that biblical prosperity is not limited to money. In fact, when I invited Jesus into my heart I became wealthy beyond measure, for I knew that God, the Creator and owner of everything, came inside me to dwell. As I have become more mature in the Lord through the years, I have also seen that the potential for supernatural wealth is limitless. As anyone becomes a better steward of what he or she already has, this act of obedience enables God to trust us with more and more of the richness in Him on every level, from His anointing to talents, opportunities, wisdom, and even material riches.

## God's Pattern for Wealth

Anyone who desires to gain a better understanding of true biblical prosperity has a treasury of proven guidelines provided throughout the Bible. You can grow into God's supernatural prosperity as you follow His directions. Let me list a few basics:

**You must acknowledge that God wants you to prosper**— *"Beloved, I wish above all things that thou mayest prosper and be in health, even as thy soul prospereth"* (3 John 2). As your soul grows and prospers, so will the rest of you. As you study the Word and apply His principles, God will give you greater prosperity.

**Tithe and give offerings**—"*Bring ye all the tithes into the store-house, that there may be meat in mine house, and prove me now herewith, saith the LORD of hosts, if I will not open you the windows of heaven, and pour you out a blessing, that there shall not be room enough to receive it*" (Malachi 3:10). The tithe is a tenth of your income, no more and no less. So you don't really "give" your tithe, since it is already His. You acknowledge His ownership of everything you possess through your tithe. Whatever you give above the tithe is your offering, which is what moves you into supernatural "more than enough" prosperity. This foundation is basic and unchangeable. Without it, the blessings from any offering—Passover or otherwise—will not be effective.

**Work so you can pay your tithe and offerings**—"*Let him that stole steal no more: but rather let him labour, working with his hands the thing which is good, that he may have to give to him that needeth*" (Ephesians 4:28). There are plenty of instructions throughout the Bible about working, including this one from Proverbs 10:4-5: "*He becometh poor that dealeth with a slack hand: but the hand of the diligent maketh rich. He that gathereth in summer is a wise son: but he that sleepeth in harvest is a son that causeth shame.*" Working should never be an end in itself, for total dependence upon the world's economic system will leave you lacking. Working enables you to give, but giving is what causes you to prosper though by the planting of your seed in anointed ground.

**Pay your covenant vows to God**—"*When thou vowest a vow unto God, defer not to pay it; for he hath no pleasure in fools: pay that which thou hast vowed*" (Ecclesiastes 5:4). Psalm 50:14 confirms: "*Offer unto God thanksgiving; and pay thy vows unto the most High.*" Deuteronomy 29:9 offers this commandment: "*Keep therefore the words of this covenant, and do them, that ye may prosper in all that ye do.*"

**Give to help others in need**—"*He that giveth unto the poor shall not lack*" (Proverbs 28:27). How would you like to have a life with no lack?

**Understand that God is the Source of your prosperity**—Throughout the Gospels, we find 176 recorded instances in which Jesus acknowledged His Father as His Source. How can we do anything less? Only God can cause supernatural wealth to flow through you. Likewise, only He can teach you how to enter the realm of supernatural prosperity: *"Thus saith the LORD, thy Redeemer, the Holy One of Israel; I am the LORD thy God which teacheth thee to profit, which leadeth thee by the way that thou shouldest go"* (Isaiah 48:17).

**Realize that the Lord can even send His angel with you to make you prosper**—*"And he said unto me, The LORD, before whom I walk, will send his angel with thee, and prosper thy way"* (Genesis 24:40). If the Lord has called you to do a thing, He will make your way prosperous: *"I, even I, have spoken; yea, I have called him: I have brought him, and he shall make his way prosperous"* (Isaiah 48:15).

**Understand how obedience brings God's blessings**—*"And all these blessings shall come on thee, and overtake thee, if thou shalt hearken unto the voice of the LORD thy God"* (Deuteronomy 28:2). The release of God's blessings in your life is connected to your obedience. In fact, obedience to God's Word is vital to your financial success, for the Bible declares: *"This book of the law shall not depart out of thy mouth; but thou shalt meditate therein day and night, that thou mayest observe to do according to all that is written therein: for then thou shalt make thy way prosperous, and then thou shalt have good success"* (Joshua 1:8).

**Ask the Lord for wisdom and understanding**—*"Only the LORD give thee wisdom and understanding, and give thee charge concerning Israel, that thou mayest keep the law of the LORD thy God. Then shalt thou prosper"* (1 Chronicles 22:12-13). God will teach you supernaturally what you don't know in the natural: *"Thus saith the LORD, thy Redeemer, the Holy One of Israel, I am the LORD thy God which teacheth thee to profit"* (Isaiah 48:17).

**Expect God to cause prosperity to come into your life**— *"But without faith it is impossible to please him: for he that cometh to God must believe that he is, and that he is a rewarder of them that diligently seek him"* (Hebrews 11:6). Just as any farmer operates, you should expect a harvest from the seed you plant. God will answer and reward you for your obedience to Him.

**Give from a cheerful heart**— *"But this I say, He which soweth sparingly shall reap also sparingly; and he which soweth bountifully shall reap also bountifully. Every man according as he purposeth in his heart, so let him give; not grudgingly, or of necessity: for God loveth a cheerful giver"* (2 Corinthians 9:6-7). God will pour out His abundant blessings on you when you give cheerfully from a generous heart.

**Give your Passover offering**—Notice in the Exodus 23:15 passage, there is a prerequisite to all the seven Passover blessings: *"None shall appear before me empty."*

I pray that you will experience God's boundless provision. I can't wait to hear reports of your life filled with "no lack blessings" promised in the Word of God, *"always having all sufficiency in all things"* (2 Corinthians 9:8).

## Kingdom Prosperity

God wants to bless you in every area of your life, including your finances. There is no limit to God's supply, for His resources are inexhaustible. *"But my God shall supply all your need according to his riches in glory by Christ Jesus"* (Philippians 4:19).

As a special blessing, God's promise of increase is also extended to you and your children. *"The LORD shall increase you more and more, you and your children"* (Psalm 115:14). God will bless and prosper you and your children when you fear and obey Him, especially in the area of finances. *"Blessed is the man that feareth the LORD, that delighteth greatly in his commandments. His seed shall be mighty upon earth: the generation of the upright shall be blessed. Wealth and riches shall be in his house"* (Psalm 112:1-3).

God can use you and your family to build a mighty heritage as you grow into deeper knowledge and wisdom: *"The LORD shall open unto thee his good treasure, the heaven to give the rain unto thy land in his season, and to bless all the work of thine hand: and thou shalt lend unto many nations, and thou shalt not borrow"* (Deuteronomy 28:12).

God has a wonderful plan for your financial future. The Bible is filled with promises of the Father's blessings for those who understand and obey the Creator's fixed laws of sowing and reaping, especially when believers also realize the importance of the Passover offering. As you apply His kingdom principles, you can live an abundant life filled with financial miracles!

What seeds are you willing to plant in order to reap a bountiful, supernatural harvest of Passover blessings?

# CHAPTER 7

# BLESSING 4:
# GOD WILL TAKE
# SICKNESS AWAY
# FROM YOU

ONE OF THE MOST EXCITING and life-changing blessings of observing the Passover is found in Exodus 23:25—*"And I will take sickness away from the midst of thee."* God will literally take illness and disease away from you.

There are numerous examples of this specific blessing. I have already mentioned the story about Hezekiah, found in 2 Chronicles 30 and 2 Kings 20. When Hezekiah became king, he reestablished the passover offering. At the time, he was thirty-nine years old and dying. God healed Hezekiah, extended his life, and killed his enemies. Hezekiah became a very wealthy man in the next fifteen years.

King David is known to have observed the Passover with his offering, and God took away the physical and mental sickness that plagued him. Notice these selected verses from Psalm 116: *"I love the LORD, because he hath heard my voice and my supplications. Because he hath inclined his ear unto me, therefore will I call upon him as long as I live.... I was greatly afflicted.... What shall I render unto the LORD for all his benefits toward me? I will take the cup of salvation, and call upon the name of the LORD. I will pay my vows unto the LORD now in the presence of all his people.... I will offer to thee the sacrifice of thanksgiving, and will call upon the name of the LORD"* (verses 1-2, 10, 12-14, 17).

Many times David acknowledged his illness and God's delivery: *"O LORD my God, I cried out to You, and You healed me"* (Psalm 30:2, NKJV).

## History's Pages

As both kings Hezekiah and David understood, God Almighty wants His children well and healthy. Divine health was always God's plan for mankind, long before the Passover blessings were established.

When we examine Adam's life in the Garden of Eden before the Fall, we find that he was healthy and had dominion over everything. Sickness entered the human race after Adam's sin. God created Adam healthy, a perfect act of creation. We find no record of sickness until after sin entered the world, but from that point we find numerous instances of people who were healed. In fact, the Bible is filled with glorious accounts of miracles.

Exodus 15:26 explains God's plan for the children of Israel: *"If thou wilt diligently hearken to the voice of the LORD thy God, and wilt do that which is right in his sight, and wilt give ear to his commandments, and keep all his statutes, I will put none of these diseases upon thee, which I have brought upon the Egyptians: for I am the LORD that healeth thee."*

Jeremiah 30:17 promises, *"'For I will restore health to you and heal you of your wounds,' says the Lord."*

The Word of the Lord declares that God sent His Son, and because Jesus came, no sickness has any legal right over you. Throughout the ministry of Jesus, Scripture reveals many occasions when He supernaturally intervened in the lives of men and women. From turning water into wine at Canaan to raising Jairus's daughter from the dead, He brought help and hope to desperate lives. There was no disease or condition that was too difficult for Jesus to heal. He had power over all diseases.

The same Jesus who walked this earth "healing all manner of sickness and all manner of disease among the people" still heals today. Diseases and infirmities still vanish as sick bodies are transformed by the healing touch of Jesus. Health and life are restored when the Master appears. His mercy brings both salvation and the miraculous. Best of all, the healing stream that flowed from the Cross flows through our lives today, especially when we understand the principles of the Passover blessings.

## Seven Purposes for Healing

Let me share seven of God's many purposes or reasons for healing people—then and now.

**Jesus heals to bring glory to His Father.** On the side of a mountain near the Sea of Galilee *"great multitudes came unto him. . .and he healed them: Insomuch that the multitude wondered, when they saw the dumb to speak, the maimed to be whole, the lame to walk, and the blind to see: and they glorified the God of Israel"* (Matthew 15:30-31). On another occasion, there was a similar response when Jesus healed a paralytic man: *"When the multitude saw it, they marvelled, and glorified God"* (Matthew 9:8). All glory and praise belongs to the Father. Healing is a wonderful, awe-inspiring faith builder that should lead to glorifying God.

**Jesus heals to fulfill God's promises.** At Capernaum *"they brought unto him many that were possessed with devils: and he cast out the spirits with his word, and healed all that were sick: That it might be fulfilled which was spoken by Esaias the prophet, saying, Himself took our infirmities, and bare our sicknesses"* (Matthew 8:16-17). When the Master heals, it is a fulfillment of the prophecy spoken through Isaiah. On the cross, Christ took our sickness and infirmities.

**Jesus heals to confirm His own Word.** Healing was promised by the Father, then declared by Jesus Christ. He said, *"If I do not the works of my Father, believe me not. But if I do, though ye believe not me, believe the works: that ye may know, and believe, that the Father is in me, and I in him"* (John 10:37-38). Christ knew exactly why He was sent to earth. He came to perform the works of His Father. Miracles confirm the spoken word of Jesus. He heals to fulfill His personal promise to you.

**Jesus heals to show you the power in His blood.** The prophecy declared in Isaiah 54:4-5 was fulfilled twenty centuries ago: *"He was bruised for our iniquities: the chastisement of our peace was upon him; and with his stripes we are healed "* (Isaiah 53:5). The blood of Jesus was shed to forgive sin and provide healing.

**Jesus heals because healing belongs to His children.** Once, when Jesus was preaching near the city of Tyre, a Syrophenician fell at His feet, asking Him to cast an unclean spirit out of her daughter. Jesus said to her, *"Let the children first be filled: for it is not meet to take the children's bread, and to cast it unto the dogs. And she answered and said unto him, Yes, Lord: yet the dogs under the table eat of the children's crumbs"* (Mark 7:27-28). The Lord saw the woman's faith and the daughter was delivered. If you are a child of the King, healing should come to you first, even before unbelievers receive their miracle. Yet I watch as those who do not know the Lord reach out in great faith, hungry for the crumbs. And time after time He pours out His healing virtue upon these people. Thank God, healing is often the entry point that helps people receive Jesus Christ as Savior.

**Jesus heals because He is full of compassion.** A leper came to Jesus *"beseeching him, and kneeling down to him, and saying unto him, If thou wilt, thou canst make me clean"* (Mark 1:40). What was the Lord's response? *"And Jesus, moved with compassion, put forth his hand, and touched him, and saith unto him, I will; be thou clean"* (1:41). It was compassion that led to the miracle. Jesus Christ heals people today for the same reason, since *"the goodness of God leadeth thee to repentance"* (Romans 2:4).

**Every time the Lord heals, He once again exposes the devil's defeat on Calvary's cross.** The Word tells us, *"For this purpose the Son of God was manifested, that he might destroy the works of the devil"* (1 John 3:8). At the house of Cornelius, Peter said, *"Ye know how God anointed Jesus of Nazareth with the Holy Ghost and with power: who went about doing good, and healing all that were oppressed of the devil; for God was with him"* (Acts 10:37-38).

"Healing is for us today," wrote A. W. Tozer, the powerful Bible teacher. "Whatever God did and was able to do and willing to do at any time, God is able and willing to do again, within the framework of His will! So what we need to do is get acquainted with God."[1]

What a blessing!

## Priceless Treasure

Jesus knows everything about you. You are His treasure. He even knows the number of hairs on your head (Matthew 10:29-31). He desires to show mercy and healing toward you. You are so precious that He died on the cross for your sin and your infirmities. Will you do whatever it takes to allow the Great Physician to bring healing and deliverance to you today?

Be faithful in observing the Passover and get ready for a supernatural life as God takes sickness away from you! Then you can offer your thanksgiving praise: Lord, by Your stripes I am healed. Thank You, Jesus, for Your shed blood that causes sickness to pass over me. In You I am well. Through You I am whole. You are the Lord who heals me!

# CHAPTER 8

# BLESSING 5:
# GOD WILL GIVE YOU A LONG LIFE

ONE OF THE MOST ASTOUNDING BLESSINGS from God's promises concerning those who honor and observe the Passover is the blessing of long life: *"I will fulfill the number of your days"* (Exodus 23:26, NKJV). In other words, you shall not die before your appointed time; you will enjoy a long life span.

This blessing is mentioned throughout the Bible. Once again, Hezekiah is an excellent example of one who experienced the blessings that come from the observance of the Passover. After he reestablished the celebration of Passover, God changed His mind about allowing Hezekiah's life to be finished at the age of thirty-nine. He lived fifteen years longer.

Granted, the Bible says that life and death are ultimately in the hands of God. However, it is quite apparent from a study of the Word that our behavior and ultimately our obedience to the Father can affect the length of our lives here on earth.

King Solomon wrote: *"The fear of the LORD prolongeth days: but the years of the wicked shall be shortened"* (Proverbs 10:27).

Also in Proverbs we are told: *"My son, forget not my law; but let thine heart keep my commandments: For length of days, and long life, and peace, shall they add to thee*" (3:1-2). The first verse points to a cause, while the second gives the effect. In other words, if we keep God's laws, three things will be produced: days full of accomplishment, long life, and peace. What wonderful promises from our Father!

Likewise, Moses gave us this clear-cut promise: "*Thou shalt keep therefore his statutes, and his commandments, which I command thee this day, that it may go well with thee, and with thy children after thee, and that thou mayest prolong thy days upon the earth, which the LORD thy God giveth thee, for ever*" (Deuteronomy 4:40).

Paul gave us this pointed truth: "*Honour thy father and mother; (which is the first commandment with promise;) That it may be well with thee, and thou mayest live long on the earth*" (Ephesians 6:2-3).

Let's look at Psalm 91:14-16: "*Because he hath set his love upon me, therefore will I deliver him: I will set him on high, because he hath known my name. He shall call upon me, and I will answer him: I will be with him in trouble; I will deliver him, and honour him. With long life will I satisfy him, and show him my salvation.*"

Obviously, the Lord wants to bless us and our families with long life and peace, just as He does with His many other blessings. Our part is to walk in faith and obedience.

## A Biblical Prescription for a Long, Abundant Life

In Deuteronomy 10:12-13, we see something very revealing: "*What doth the LORD thy God require of thee, but to fear the LORD thy God, to walk in all his ways, and to love him, and to serve the LORD thy God with all thy heart and with all thy soul, to keep the commandments of the LORD, and his statutes, which I command thee this day for thy good?*"

We are told that all God's laws are given for our own good, to preserve, and shelter our lives. He certainly knows what is best for us and wisdom demands that we seek to understand His laws that lead to a long, abundant life.

Consider obedience to our parents: *"Children, obey your parents in the Lord"* (Ephesians 6:1). There is something about honoring parents that causes things to go well for us and extends our lives. After years of pastoral counseling, I've seen this principle at work in so many areas of life. Those who fail to honor parents also, for example, will likely fail to honor and respect other authorities.

Here is another basic principle of long life. In Proverbs 3:1-6, we read these sobering instructions:

> *My son, forget not my law; but let thine heart keep my commandments: For length of days, and long life, and peace, shall they add to thee. Let not mercy and truth forsake thee: bind them about thy neck; write them upon the table of thine heart: So shalt thou find favour and good understanding in the sight of God and man. Trust in the LORD with all thine heart; and lean not unto thine own understanding. In all thy ways acknowledge him, and he shall direct thy paths.*

Keeping God's commands will add long life and so much more!

## God Will Fill Your Life with More Than Enough

The Bible mentions "no lack" in both the Old and New Testaments. Deuteronomy 8:9 talks of possessing *"A land wherein thou shalt eat bread without scarceness, thou shalt not lack any thing in it; a land whose stones are iron, and out of whose hills thou mayest dig brass."* This passage in Thessalonians declares: *"That ye may have lack of nothing"* (4:12).

When the Scriptures talk about "no lack," they hold before us the prospect of having all of our needs met. It is important to realize that this just begins to scratch the surface in describing the kind of blessing the Father bestows upon His obedient children. Remember, there is no scarcity with God. He doesn't need to ration blessings so that He will have enough to go around. In fact, when we enjoy biblical abundance, we experience what the apostle Paul spoke of in 2 Corinthians 9:8-11:

*And God is able to make all grace abound to you, so that in all things at all times, having all that you need, you will abound in every good work. As it is written: "He has scattered abroad his gifts to the poor; his righteousness endures forever." Now he who supplies seed to the sower and bread for food will also supply and increase your store of seed and will enlarge the harvest of your righteousness. You will be made rich in every way so that you can be generous on every occasion, and through us your generosity will result in thanksgiving to God* (NIV).

## God Will Fill Your Life with Blessings That Cannot Be Bought

When we are obedient to God, we can know an abundance that people who have not accepted the Savior simply cannot understand. Not one of these mighty blessings on the following list can be purchased, yet all of them are part of true biblical prosperity and come from the gracious hand of our wonderful, prospering Lord!

**Salvation**—*"For God so loved the world, that he gave his only begotten Son, that whosoever believeth in him should not perish, but have everlasting life"* (John 3:16).

**Health**—*"Who forgiveth all thine iniquities; who healeth all thy diseases"* (Psalm 103:3).

**Deliverance**—*"He delivered me from my strong enemy, and from them which hated me: for they were too strong for me"* (Psalm 18:17).

**Strength**—*"The LORD is my rock, and my fortress, and my deliverer; my God, my strength, in whom I will trust; my buckler, and the horn of my salvation, and my high tower"* (Psalm 18:2).

**Protection**—*"For the eyes of the LORD run to and fro throughout the whole earth, to shew himself strong in the behalf of them whose heart is perfect toward him. Herein thou hast done foolishly: therefore from henceforth thou shalt have wars"* (2 Chronicles 16:9).

**Answers to prayer**—*"Now know I that the LORD saveth his anointed; he will hear him from his holy heaven with the saving strength of his right hand"* (Psalm 20:6).

**Victory**—*"But thanks be to God, which giveth us the victory through our Lord Jesus Christ"* (1 Corinthians 15:57).

**Preservation**—*"The LORD preserveth all them that love him: but all the wicked will he destroy"* (Psalm 145:20).

**Reward**—*"If any man's work abide which he hath built thereupon, he shall receive a reward"* (1 Corinthians 3:14).

**Eternal Inheritance**—*"The LORD knoweth the days of the upright: and their inheritance shall be for ever"* (Psalm 37:18).

## God Gives a Life of Abundance

You see, God has a plan and a purpose for every human being in this world. It is a wonderful plan, and He promises His children a long life so that we can fulfill it. However, we do have an enemy, the devil, who is out to destroy that plan along with God's purpose for our lives. Jesus spoke of the devil as a robber who seeks to take away peace and our promised long lives: *"The thief cometh not, but for to steal, and to kill, and to destroy: I am come that they might have life, and that they might have it more abundantly"* (John 10:10).

Abundance means so much more than wealth or prosperity. Abundance brings the abiding presence of the Lord Jesus into your life. Jesus makes all the difference! When you know Jesus Christ and have a personal relationship with Him, you have ample amounts, great supplies, and full measures of blessings. He is the more-than-enough God. He provides plenty—a surplus, a heap, a bounty of blessings that overtakes believers who understand how to operate in the miraculous. Knowing Him and having a personal relationship with Jesus Christ is the greatest blessing a person can know, not only in this life, but in the eternal life to come. I love the truth expressed in Bill Gaither's memorable song:

The longer I serve Him the sweeter He grows,
The more that I love Him, more love He bestows;

Each day is like heaven, my heart overflows,
The longer I serve Him the sweeter He grows.[1]

The lines of that song speak of the abundance that our heavenly Father holds before each of us today and why it is so unfortunate when people spend so much time looking for material blessing that they overlook all the other manifestations of God's blessing happening around them. Worse than that, when people obsess on riches and seek only material wealth, they limit God because of their mistaken notion of what will bring happiness to their lives. True happiness comes only through surrender to the Father's will. When I surrender to Him, I will be blessed; He has promised to take care of me, and I know He will!

## Blessings Through You and to You

The late Dr. E. V. Hill, a great preacher and dynamic man of God, once made this powerful statement: "If God can get it *through* you, God can get it *to* you." There is such wisdom in this statement.

You see, on the one hand, the Lord doesn't bless us so we can merely consume what we receive. Yet, the Lord doesn't expect us just to be hardened pipelines for blessings to flow through us to others, never experiencing the blessings ourselves. There is a balance from Scripture. When we are obedient to the Father, we use all that He gives us to bless others. And then because we are obedient children, the Father delights in blessing us. Those blessings, as we are obedient in our observance of the Passover and all other areas of our Christian walk, include a long, filled life!

God wants to bless you far more than you want to be blessed! It can be comforting to believers today that God's love for His children and His willingness to bless were clearly illustrated in His dealings with the children of Israel. His faithfulness to them year after year extended into every aspect of their lives, even to the point that their shoes never wore out while they walked forty years in the wilderness. The promises of God to the children of Israel certainly extend to you and me as His children today, and our loving heavenly Father promises to His children a testimony of His faithfulness as He seeks to bless generation after generation as we build up a mighty heritage!

To believe in the Lord Jesus and follow Him in simple obedience to His Word— including the observance of the Passover— offers a special promise of happiness, health, blessings, and a long, abundant life. Faith in *"the Lamb of God, which taketh away the sin of the world"* (John 1:29) will also give us eternal life in the world hereafter!

# CHAPTER 9

# BLESSING 6:
# GOD WILL CAUSE INCREASE AND INHERITANCE

E XODUS 23:30 PROCLAIMS to those who honor the Passover to increase and inheritance will be yours. But what does that involve?

To the children of Israel, it meant this: *"And I will bring you in unto the land, concerning the which I did swear to give it to Abraham, to Isaac, and to Jacob; and I will give it you for an heritage: I am the LORD"* (Exodus 6:8).

*Heritage* and *inheritance* come from the same root word. "Increase and inheritance" means that you need to get ready to be blessed far beyond anything you can imagine. God will cause affluence to come into the life of the Passover celebrant in the form of nonwage prosperity. God promised that we would receive an inheritance, which is something we obtain through position, not something we work to acquire!

How would your life change if you truly began to receive the inheritance God has provided for you?

## God's Blessing of Inheritance

Dwight Moody was one of history's most influential and effective servants of God. He describes what happened as he sought a deeper walk with Lord: "I was crying all the time that God would fill me with His Spirit. Well, one day, in the city of New York—oh, what a day! I cannot describe it. I seldom refer to it; it is almost too sacred an experience to name. I can only say that God revealed Himself to me, and I had such an experience of His love that I had to ask Him to stay His hand." [1]

The abundant, inheritance-filled life is truly amazing. The Word of God promises that *"blessings shall come on thee, and overtake thee"* (Deuteronomy 28:2). We have embraced so little of what God has promised us. We must begin to think the way that God wants us to think and receive His promises in our lives.

We have so much treasure, on the inside and outside, just waiting to flourish and blossom into a powerful harvest. Bill Swad, a special man whom God has blessed abundantly, has given generously through the years to the work of the Lord. He says, "The seeds God has planted in your life are not there by accident. They are an important part of His great plan for your future." Are you ready to see a harvest from the seeds God has planted inside you, seeds which may have been dormant all of your life? Are you ready for a special blessing of increase and inheritance?

It's time to rise up! God's people are a mighty people. We must get the world's idea of loss and lack out of our minds. As a Christian, you are under a completely different umbrella or covering, than those who have not accepted the Lord Jesus in their life. God's blessing is yours by promise. You may ask, "How then, do I obtain the promises?" You simply obey His word and act in faith as a blood-bought child of God! When you do, especially as you understand and apply the blessing of Passover, you will begin to experience a dynamic principle of receiving nonwage prosperity.

God's will is that you will never lack in any area of your life. He said, *"My people shall never be ashamed"* (Joel 2:26). I believe with all of my heart that is exactly what God has promised His own.

It is up to us as His people to prepare our lives by increasing our capacity to receive God's abiding and abundant grace. Isaiah says you do that by enlarging the place of your tent, stretching out the curtains of your habitation, lengthening your cords, and strengthening your stakes. In other words, prepare your heart to receive God's abundance: *"For thou shalt break forth on the right hand and on the left; and thy seed shall inherit the Gentiles, and make the desolate cities to be inhabited"* (Isaiah 54:3). God's Word declares that recovery, restoration, and abundance belong to you!

## Going Forward

When you are under the umbrella of God's blessing of increase and inheritance, you are in drive, not reverse. In Christ, everything about you goes forward, not backward. The moment you come under the umbrella of God's presence, and the very second you are in Christ, everything about you begins to change. Increase is the outcome of the life of Christ in you.

The Christian life is an ever-expanding life moving from life into deeper life. The Greek word for this expanding power is *dunamis*, which means "power reproducing itself within itself." The power of God causes the Christian life to be a journey that continues to grow outward and become a blessing to all that it touches. It is like light that originates from one spot and shines in every direction.

Christians should continually be expanding. We should live under the shower of blessings: *"And I will make them and the places round about my hill a blessing; and I will cause the shower to come down in his season; there shall be showers of blessing"* (Ezekiel 34:26). What an inheritance! As the power of God touches your life, He blesses with an abundant life.

Joy expands this same way as you understand increase and inheritance. As you keep God's commandments and abide in His love, His joy will be in you so that your joy will be full. However, joy does not stop there. First Peter 1:8 says that you will have *"joy unspeakable and full of glory."* God wants to see you filled to capacity and brimming over with blessings as His child.

The Bible also declares that glory expands within you. Second Corinthians 3:18 says, *"But we all, with open face beholding as in a glass the glory of the Lord, are changed into the same image from glory to glory, even as by the Spirit of the Lord."* Glory will increase in your life as you behold the Lord and are affected by His presence. The process of growth continues until one day when you are in eternal glory with the Lord. God wants you to be surrounded with expanding, intensifying, and thickening life, joy, and glory.

## Flowing in Your Inheritance

We are changed into the image of the Lord continually as we understand the blessing of increase and inheritance. Colossians 3:10 says, *"Put on the new man, which is renewed in knowledge after the image of him that created him."* This verse describes moving transformation and ongoing re-creation.

These blessing happen in your life as you come into the flow of the Holy Ghost, which will carry you from glory to glory in God. Eventually, in heaven, you will reach the place of fullness and totality, but God wants the process of abundance to begin in you right now. He wants you to enjoy your heritage now as a child of God as you move forward in faith!

## Faith and Inheritance

Faith is acting upon your belief in God. Faith believes Him not just in words, but also in deed. If faith is not acting and alive, it is not faith. Luke 16:16 says, *"The law and the prophets were until John: since that time the kingdom of God is preached, and every man presseth into it."* You press into God's kingdom by taking hold of the heritage you have already received.

It's time to embrace the promises of God in your life. I love what Hebrews 11:13 says, *"These all died in faith, not having received the promises, but having seen them afar off, and were persuaded of them, and embraced them, and confessed that they were strangers and pilgrims on the earth."* As part of your inheritance as a child of God, you can actually take the Father's promises and press them close to your heart so that they will never escape you.

As you combine your faith with works you will see every promise God has made within your heart come to pass, for faith always has a destination. Faith is going somewhere and you are going there too when you put your whole heart into believing the precious promises in God's Word.

With the heart, man believeth, and with the mouth, confession is made. That is a moving faith with a destination. That is faith that is born in the heart and coming out of the life. Faith then moves out of the life and has a destination. Faith never stays locked up inside. It goes from your heart, to your mouth (or speech), and then shows in your life.

## The Price

I heard the following story when I was very young. I don't know if it is true or not, but it made such an impression, then and now, that I want to share it with you.

A young man from a farming region of England decided to come to America, but his family was extremely poor. Still, over a period of time, he was able to scrimp and save enough for the price of a ticket. Finally, he said his farewells to family and friends, threw a small sack of belongings over his back, and began walking toward the port where he would depart for his new life.

When he arrived at the ship's ticket office, he was dismayed to discover that the price of the ticket had been increased. It took nearly every bit of the money he had saved to purchase the ticket. Undaunted, he determined to go ahead, even if he had nothing much left for food or supplies on the ship.

Day after day, as the ship crossed the Atlantic, he dreamed of the day he would arrive in New York City. He imagined what he would do. His dreams kept him going, even as his food supplies ran out. Days turned into weeks. He used the last of his money to buy a few more things to eat. By that time he had grown gaunt from impending starvation.

One day the ship's captain happened to see the increasingly slender youth and asked, "Where have you been keeping yourself? I haven't seen you at any of the meals. Why don't you sit at my table this evening as my guest?"

Embarrassed, the young man hesitated. Finally he admitted, "I have no more money for food. I cannot come to dinner with you tonight. I'm sorry."

"No money!" the captain exclaimed. "You don't need money. All the food you can eat was paid for when you purchased your ticket!"

Needless to say, the young man enjoyed the next meal beyond measure. And the next. And the next. By the time he arrived in New York harbor, he had more than gained back the weight he had lost during the trip. Too bad he wasted the first half of the trip, not knowing that everything, including the food, had been bought with the price of his ticket.

## Purchased with the Ultimate Price

Just as with the illustration of the young man on his journey to a new life, Christians simply fail to understand all that was bought when the Lamb of God became our Passover, our Deliverer, and our Savior. For too long, the devil's success has been dependent upon Christians' lack of knowledge. The Bible declares, *"My people are destroyed for lack of knowledge"* (Hosea 4:6). You must know what the Bible says so you can move forward in faith to claim your inheritance.

Please understand that hope and faith are two entirely different things. The Scriptures say that "faith is the substance of things hoped for" (Hebrews 11:1). Why? Because hope takes care of tomorrow, and faith takes care of today. Hope is always in the future. It is in the mind, not in the heart. Hope is good, but it must not be confused with faith. Some people say, "Oh, I hope so." That is nice, but "hoping so" is not faith. Hope deals with tomorrow, or the future, and faith deals with today, or the present.

Faith comes from the heart and is produced by the Holy Ghost, by hearing the Word of God. Romans 10:10 says, *"For with the heart man believeth unto righteousness; and with the mouth confession is made unto salvation."* With the heart, man believeth. Heart faith becomes a part of you as you understand more and more what it means to be a blood-bought child of God.

Smith Wigglesworth once wrote:

> Faith is the Word of God. It is the personal inward flow of divine favor, which moves in every fiber of our being until our whole nature is so quickened that we live by faith, we move by faith, and we are going to be caught up to glory by faith, for faith is the victory! Faith is the glorious knowledge of a personal presence within you, changing you from strength to strength, from glory to glory, until you get to the place where you walk with God, and God thinks and speaks through you by the power of the Holy Spirit.[2]

## Inherited Treasure

For great results to come out of your life, you must hear the Word of God, read the Word, protect the Word, keep the Word, and make sure your life is filled with the Word. Proverbs 4:20-22 says, *"My son, attend to my words; incline thine ear unto my sayings. Let them not depart from thine eyes; keep them in the midst of thine heart. For they are life unto those that find them, and health to all their flesh."*

As you build your life upon God's Word, understanding and accessing your inheritance will be a natural outcome. Prayer and meditation upon God's Word activates your faith. James 4:2 says, *"Ye have not, because ye ask not."* Faith is not faith until it expects an answer. The psalmist said, *"My voice shalt thou hear in the morning, O LORD; in the morning will I direct my prayer unto thee, and will look up"* (Psalm 5:3). "Will look up" means that he is expecting an answer to his prayers.

As you begin to understand increase and inheritance in your life as one of the blessings of honoring Passover, you can pray in full assurance that God will hear and answer you. James 1:6 says, *"But let him ask in faith, nothing wavering. For he that wavereth is like a wave of the sea driven with the wind and tossed."*

Romans 10:17 says, *"So then faith cometh by hearing, and hearing by the word of God."* As you read the Word, the Spirit of God will put life into that *logos* word (the written Word of God; knowledge of the Word), and it will become a *rhema* word (a precise, quickened direction of Scripture for a particular person or circumstance, given by the Holy Spirit and brought to remembrance for use in times of special need) in your soul. At that point, the Word becomes alive, and it has living faith for you as part of your inheritance.

## Above and Not Beneath

Isaiah 60:1 exhorts, *"Arise, shine; for thy light is come, and the glory of the LORD is risen upon thee."* God wants you to be the head, not the tail. God declared through Moses that you should be a lender, not a borrower. You are above, not beneath. You are a person of victory, not defeat. What an inheritance!

You can arise today and claim your increase and inheritance in Christ. After all, the Word of God is filled with promise after promise of your inheritance. God wants to see you blessed in every area of your life. He intends for you to live abundantly today, anointed and highly favored.

Smith Wigglesworth, a great man of faith said, "There is only one way to all the treasures of God, and that is the way of faith. All things are possible, even the fulfilling of all promises is possible, to him who believes."[3]

Second Corinthians 5:7 says, *"For we walk by faith, not by sight."* Another mighty promise is found in 1 John 5:4, which says, *"For whatsoever is born of God overcometh the world: and this is the victory that overcometh the world, even our faith."*

Our inheritance even includes protection: *"No weapon that is formed against thee shall prosper; and every tongue that shall rise against thee in judgment thou shalt condemn. This is the heritage of the servants of the LORD, and their righteousness is of me, saith the LORD"* (Isaiah 54:17).

What an inheritance! What a legacy!

# CHAPTER 10

# BLESSING 7:
# GOD WILL GIVE
# A SPECIAL YEAR
# OF BLESSING

E XODUS 23 OFFERS SEVERAL VERSES that explain how God will give a special year of blessing as a result of honoring Passover: *"And I will set thy bounds from the Red sea even unto the sea of the Philistines, and from the desert unto the river: for I will deliver the inhabitants of the land into your hand; and thou shalt drive them out before thee"* (23:31). What the enemy stole will be returned to you and protected by God from being overtaken: *"I will not drive them out from before thee in one year; lest the land become desolate, and the beast of the field multiply against thee"* (23:29).

God sets schedules and time boundaries for His feasts. He instructed, *"Three times you shall keep a feast to Me"* (Exodus 23:14, NKJV). In Exodus 23, he promised that the blessings He would give to His people would remain in place for an entire year. That same blessing is available to us today, for the Lamb of God whom we serve is *"Jesus Christ the same yesterday, and to day, and for ever* (Hebrews 13:8).

## Your Promise

You see, since the day that you became a Christian, the power of God has been working in you to reverse what the devil has stolen. First Corinthians 15:22 says, *"For as in Adam all die, even so in Christ shall all be made alive."* Adam was created by God to stay alive, yet Adam went from life to death, and since then all men have gone from life to death. Through Jesus Christ, we can go from death to life. Romans 8:2 says, *"For the law of the Spirit of life in Christ Jesus hath made me free from the law of sin and death."*

God's children live under a different structure and set of guidelines than the world does. We live in the spirit, not the flesh.

The world says a person begins to die the moment he or she is born, but God says: *"Therefore if any man be in Christ, he is a new creature: old things are passed away; behold, all things are become new"* (2 Corinthians 5:17). God gives life!

The world believes that people wear out, but God promises, *"Though our outward man perish, yet the inward man is renewed day by day"* (2 Corinthians 4:16). We serve the God who makes all things new. And that is just the beginning!

## Lost and Found

When you are in Christ a dynamic (*dunamis*) power begins to be unleashed in your life. Before you gave your life to the Lord, you were going one way, being pulled in one direction by an evil force. That evil force pulls people away from the cross and into darkness and bondage.

But when Jesus enters a life, God changes it from lost to saved, from dying to living, and from despondency to joy. Psalm 30:11 says, *"Thou hast turned for me my mourning into dancing."* You can rejoice continually, for God has redeemed your life from certain destruction!

Things change dramatically when you obey and serve God. As your life is filled with God's Word and you act upon your faith, you will have the authority to take back what the enemy took. Legally, it is your right to reclaim what is yours.

God Word says that the enemy of your soul is a thief. Did you know that Scripture states clearly that the enemy must restore double what he has taken from you:*"If the theft be certainly found in his hand alive, whether it be ox, or ass, or sheep; he shall restore double"* (Exodus 22:4). The thief must give back double restitution.

The devil must pay you back double for what you have lost. Is that a great nonwage blessing or what? Our God is the God of the lost and found. This is your season and promised year of blessing and recovery.

## No Loss, Only Gain

It is amazing how we Christians have been sold such a "bill of goods." We think we have to give up so much to obey and serve our Father, but nothing could be further from the truth. Nothing is lost when you serve Jesus. The Lord Jesus promised that *"every one that hath forsaken houses, or brethren, or sisters, or father, or mother, or wife, or children, or lands, for my name's sake, shall receive an hundredfold, and shall inherit everlasting life"* (Matthew 19:29). God will command His blessings upon you when your commitment to Him is steadfast and true.

God said that if you serve Him, *"He will bless your bread and your water; and take sickness away from the midst of you"* (Exodus 23:25, NKJV). As you abide in Christ, God will multiply, keep, protect, and watch over you. He will drive the enemy away from you.

Think about Job, for example, who thought that he lost everything, yet he recovered it all. Even though Job was at his lowest point, he prayed, *"I know that thou canst do every thing, and that no thought can be withholden from thee"* (Job 42:2). Job's trust in the Lord remained strong and true despite his circumstances. The Lord was pleased with Job, and replaced double everything that was taken from him: *"And the LORD turned the captivity of Job, when he prayed for his friends: also the Lord gave Job twice as much as he had before"* (Job 42:10).

The Word of God goes on to say, *"The Lord blessed the latter end of Job more than his beginning"* (Job 42:12). Because Job trusted in the Lord, God gave him more in the end than he had in the beginning.

## This Land Is Your Land

Are you ready to receive double of all that the devil has stolen from you? If you truly want to receive the blessings from Christ, you must go in and possess the land. Deuteronomy 2:31 says, *"And the LORD said unto me, Behold, I have begun to give Sihon and his land before thee: begin to possess, that thou mayest inherit his land."* God cannot begin giving until you start moving. After all, *"faith without works is dead"* (James 2:26). You must act upon your faith.

God will take care of the enemy in your way, but once He gives you the land, you must go and possess it. You must stand upon the ground, spiritual or physical. If it is a mountain-top, climb over the rocks and obstacles through the power in God's Word. Just as the Lord went before the children of Israel, so He will go before you.

When you act upon your faith, you begin to possess what you have inherited. In truth, you cannot inherit until you take owner-ship. You must move forward in faith, and in order to go ahead, you must forget the past. You cannot go back and change it anyway.

Besides, faith is a present-tense word, so have faith now. In the past, you may have been abused, pushed back, and told that you would not make it, but you must forget the past and start fresh now. You do that by placing your faith in what God's Word says about you. God has given you amazing promises in His Word to hold on to that will renew your mind and your spirit, if only you will activate your faith to believe what He says.

The devil will continue to oppose you as you serve the Lord, but 2 Corinthians 4:17 encourages, *"For our light affliction, which is but for a moment, worketh for us a far more exceeding and eternal weight of glory.*" Don't let the enemy discourage you as you face obstacles, battles, and attacks. After Abraham patiently endured, he *"obtained the promise"* (Hebrews 6:15). You will obtain your promise too, if you persist in Christ Jesus.

When you understand the promise of Exodus 23:29, you will also begin to realize the blessing of restoration and abundance for you. Restoration and your one-year blessing is not something you merely hope for. It is a fact. It is the promise of God.

What does this mean? You get to regain all that has been stolen from you. You are on the right side now as you serve the One whose name is above every name, the Lord Jesus! Through Him you regain your strength; you are restored to health, rescued from destruction, become established in God's kingdom. You are made new; you redeem lost time; you are refreshed, replenished, and revived!

Joel 2:23-26 contains a glorious promise:

> *Be glad then, ye children of Zion, and rejoice in the LORD your God: for he hath given you the former rain moderately, and he will cause to come down for you the rain, the former rain, and the latter rain in the first month. And the floors shall be full of wheat, and the fats shall overflow with wine and oil. And I will restore to you the years that the locust hath eaten, the cankerworm, and the caterpiller, and the palmerworm, my great army which I sent among you. And ye shall eat in plenty, and be satisfied, and praise the name of the LORD your God, that hath dealt wondrously with you: and my people shall never be ashamed.*

## The Bible Is a Book of Restoration

The Bible itself is a book of recovery and restoration. The entire Word of God is the story of God recovering man after the Fall. God created man and woman in abundance, placed them in a lush garden where they had all that they could ever want or need, and yet they fell away from the Lord and began to live in sin. Adam lost all; and Christ came to restore what was lost.

Your own life is also a story of restoration. Once you were lost, and now you are found. Once you were blind, and now you can see. Your own testimony is one of recovery, since the second you became a Christian, you came under the covering of Jesus's blood. All the blessings of Passover (and more!) became yours. Legally!

The Lord has already performed the promises in His Word for you, so why should restoration be a foreign thing to you? God's love for you is so great that He has been leading you, even while you did not know how much you needed to be rescued from sin and destruction.

Charles Finney, one of the great Christian classic writers of the 1800s and a preacher with powerful conviction, said, "God's love is not based on His being satisfied with us or having a high opinion of us. There is no basis in us for such a love. Thus, God's love can be nothing but the love of unselfish benevolence."[1]

You have escaped bondage and have been born into glorious freedom. It is time that you accept all He has for you—not just with one year's blessing, but throughout your life—simply because the Lord has so much more that He wants to give you each day.

There is no greater abundance than you will find in Christ. The Lord will be faithful to restore all to you as you walk with Him. No destructive force on this earth can ever take the true riches of His kingdom away from you. God created you to have success, to subdue your enemies, and to attain His promises.

It begins with your one year of special Passover blessing, and your obedience in the future can mean that you will go from glory to glory, year after year, in a place of great restoration and abundance!

# PART THREE

*Greater Things*

# A BETTER COVENANT

A S WITH THE SEVEN BLESSINGS of the Passover, whatever God promised to His covenant people in the Old Testament holds true for New Testament believers, those covered by the "better covenant" spoken about throughout the book of Hebrews:

> *Now of the things which we have spoken this is the sum: We have such an high priest, who is set on the right hand of the throne of the Majesty in the heavens; A minister of the sanctuary, and of the true tabernacle, which the Lord pitched, and not man....*
>
> *Who serve unto the example and shadow of heavenly things, as Moses was admonished of God when he was about to make the tabernacle.... But now hath he obtained a more excellent ministry, by how much also he is the mediator of a better covenant, which was established upon better promises.*
>
> *For if that first covenant had been faultless, then should no place have been sought for the second.* (Hebrews 8:1-2, 5-7)

Look also in Hebrews 12:24, where we are pointed toward *"Jesus the mediator of the new covenant, and to the blood of sprinkling, that speaketh better things."*

The children of Israel were told that their deliverance was dependent upon a blood covenant: *"And when I see the blood, I will pass over you"* (Exodus 12:13). Nearly three and a half centuries later, we are confronted, not with the blood of bulls and goats, but rather with the blood of Jesus, *"the Lamb of God, which taketh away the sin of the world"* (John 1:29).

During the Old Covenant, almost every sacrifice included the sprinkling or smearing of blood on the altar or within the tabernacle: *"And almost all things are by the law purged with blood; and without shedding of blood is no remission"* (Hebrews 9:22). The blood sacrifice of the Old Testament pointed toward the Lamb of God who shed His blood for the sins of the world:

> *Neither by the blood of goats and calves, but by his own blood he entered in once into the holy place, having obtained eternal redemption for us. For if the blood of bulls and of goats, and the ashes of an heifer sprinkling the unclean, sanctifieth to the purifying of the flesh: How much more shall the blood of Christ, who through the eternal Spirit offered himself without spot to God, purge your conscience from dead works to serve the living God?* (Hebrews 9:12-14)

Without the blood of Jesus there can be no eternal life for man; Jesus confirmed the validity of Leviticus when He cried out:

> *I am the living bread that came down from heaven. If anyone eats of this bread, he will live forever. This bread is my flesh, which I will give for the life of the world." Then the Jews began to argue sharply among themselves, "How can this man give us his flesh to eat?" Jesus said to them, "I tell you the truth, unless you eat the flesh of the Son of Man and drink his blood, you have no life in you"* (John 6:51-53, NIV).

The Israelites were instructed to kill a lamb and to smear the blood upon the sides and tops of the door frames. Today, as part of the "better covenant," the blood of Christ was shed to purchase salvation for anyone who calls upon His name.

God provided and offered the sacrifice—Jesus. I'm wondering, what does the blood of Christ mean to you? It would be tragic for any reader of this book to get this far in a study of the Passover blessings, yet not know the Savior who gave His life as a sacrifice for the sins of all mankind.

## Blood Covenant

Did you see Mel Gibson's film, *The Passion of the Christ*, or his later version, *The Passion Recut*? That movie literally changed my life.

People everywhere seemed to say the same thing after seeing the film. The scenes remain unforgettable to me. He literally gasped and sobbed in Gethsemane, doing battle with Satan.

When Judas kissed Him, the look in the eyes of Jesus could not be explained with words. He said, "Do you betray the Son of Man with a kiss?"

After Peter's third and final denial, no one can describe the face of the Savior as he glanced toward His defeated disciple, revealing a heart filled with such deep disappointment and utter sadness, so much so that Peter broke down in sobs of self-hatred.

Jesus's body was beaten, bloody and dirty, almost beyond recognition, with matted hair and ripped garments.

It's a motion picture that doesn't allow you to be a spectator. It engulfs you completely. Everywhere, the response—then and now—has been the same. When I saw a private preview then later saw it in a packed theater, no one clapped. People sat sobbing. It was like no one knew what to do. You just knew that your life would never be the same.

In theaters, total strangers walked up to each other, hugging, praying together. It was the most remarkable thing I've seen.

So many people told me pretty much the same thing: "I went to the movie only to see what all the controversy was about. I still don't know exactly what I believe, but I do know that something touched me very deeply while I watched the screen, and I feel compelled to begin asking questions I never wanted to ask before."

To his credit, Mel Gibson did what nearly everyone said couldn't be done. Despite breaking many of Hollywood's cherished traditions and the sometimes-gleeful doomsday predictions of virtually every film marketing expert around the globe, this blockbuster movie will undoubtedly be viewed historically as a major watershed event. Not only has it become one of the biggest theatrical moneymakers of all time, by any standard, it has also touched a worldwide nerve across all cultural boundaries, causing intense and outspoken thoughts by virtually everyone who viewed its brutal torture scenes. It continues to trigger these forceful feelings around the world, from world leaders to next-door neighbors and workplace people with whom you talk every day. And if the impact has not been monstrous enough, the movie will certainly become a must-see cinematic classic, year after year, especially during the Easter season.

Dr. Billy Graham spoke point-blank about the film: "Every time I preach or speak about the Cross, the things I saw on the screen will be on my heart and mind."

During decades to come, I believe people will look back and long remember this stunning motion picture, not just for its startling realism and heinous depictions of man's hatred and brutality toward the Son of God, but for the fact that people all over the world, as a result of seeing and experiencing *Passion*, realized how little they knew about what they were seeing on the big screen.

As I mentioned, I first went to a screening of the motion picture. Most of the people, if not all, were believers. It was moving beyond words, so stunning. Like me, most people there were simply overwhelmed at the end.

Mel Gibson, the man who invested his own $30 million and years of his time to make this motion picture, doing what he openly says was "what the Holy Spirit called me to do," has shared candidly, "This is a story about love, hope, faith, and forgiveness.

Jesus died for all mankind, suffered for all of us. It's time to get back to that basic message."

Up to the point when the movie was released, the story of Christ's crucifixion had perhaps become so familiar to both believers and nonbelievers that it had sometimes lost its ability to outrage, grieve, or even stir any great emotion. In *The Passion of the Christ*, Gibson presented history's pivotal moment in a heartrending way that absolutely forced viewers to witness every smashing blow of the whip, every slow-motion second of the savage thrust of the spear into Jesus side and every nuance of the supernatural love poured out among mankind throughout the crucifixion. Today, on the big screen or your television, you cannot help but relive history's most horrific injustice, as well as the unvarnished triumph of God's plan to reveal the sovereignty of God, expressed two centuries ago through the Holy Spirit–inspired words of John's Gospel: *"Behold the Lamb of God, which taketh away the sin of the world"* (1:29).

## Passion

Let me hasten to say that this chapter isn't about the movie. Granted, it's about the Christ of that Passion, yet that is just the beginning. The movie takes us to the Cross and Resurrection, then takes us to the moment when Jesus went to heaven to sit at the right hand of Father God. However, quite on purpose, viewers are left with an eternity-sized volume of questions, as it was intended.

The movie was produced masterfully, with a clear intent to compel people to seek answers afterward to the facts of the Savior's death that have been ignored or viewed previously through jaundiced eyes. Most people who have seen the turbulent scenes in the movie seemed unsure how to respond to such emotion-wrought images of the final twelve hours of the Son of Man. Questions remain, as they should, from such a vivid portrayal of history's most important moments.

I went into the movie with certain expectations. I'm third generation Christian. My father was a minister. My family is filled with ministers. I've been a minister most of my life. I'll admit, no matter how hard you try not to, it's easy to get familiar and perhaps even jaded about the whole subject of Jesus dying on the cross. Sure, we talk about His death, burial, and resurrection. We rejoice at Easter with songs and drama. I've written and produced major passion plays, so I've done more research and preparation than many people. But nothing prepared me for *The Passion of the Christ*. Nothing! I sat for a long time, along with many others in the screening room, and I realized that I knew nothing, compared to what I had just seen, about the depth of love Jesus revealed when He went to Calvary. It literally changed my life, for I knew that I needed to plunge into the Word to discover, for the first time in a sense, the true meaning of God's love.

## Passover, Passion, and You

I thought it was remarkable that Mel Gibson chose to make a curious cameo appearance in *The Passion of the Christ*. You never saw his face in the crowds clustered on the dusty streets of Jerusalem or on Golgotha's hill. Instead, the director decided to use his hands to nail the spikes into Jesus's hands. Admittedly, it's grotesquely difficult to watch, but in that one special scene, the moviemaker gave extraordinary insight into the true meaning of the Cross: Each of us are guilty. The results are disastrous and eternal, as Romans 6:23 states so vividly: *"For the wages of sin is death; but the gift of God is eternal life through Jesus Christ our Lord."*

Our sins, individually and collectively, nailed the perfect Son of God to the rugged timbers. Our overpowering guilt caused the Lamb of God to leave heaven to come to earth to live without sin, then to die on Calvary's cross as a sacrifice for the sins of every man, woman, and child who has ever lived or will ever live. Each of us, as Mel Gibson's hands portrayed, share the guilt. That knowledge is absolutely necessary to understanding what we must do to accept all that Christ Jesus died so that we might receive the greatest Passover blessing of all.

## A Personal Invitation

Perhaps you have been a dedicated Christian longer than I've been alive. Others, perhaps you, have never heard the Gospel before and are desperately seeking answers for questions you thought you'd never be asking until you saw *The Passion of the Christ,* picked up this book, or until God opened some other gateway to your heart.

Still, here is a basic starting point for everyone: Regardless of your background, education, or culture, the first step toward a life of forgiveness and eternity in heaven is making sure you have the Lamb of God living in your heart.

No matter what situation or set of challenges you face at this exact moment, God wants to give you the answers to all the questions you face. He gave His own Son to offer freedom from guilt and a peace that the world cannot give. The Creator of the universe offered Jesus Christ as the *"lamb of God who taketh away the sins of the world"* (John 1:29) so He could draw each of us to Himself. That's how much He cared, still cares, will care for you and me. We do not have to feel alienated or separated from Him. He wants to be in close fellowship with us.

It is a historical fact that He died on the cross and rose from the grave. By those supernatural acts, Jesus Christ paid the penalty for our sin and rebellion against God. He alone bridges the gap between God and man. John 3:16, in fact, relates: *"For God so loved the world that he gave his only begotten Son, that whosoever believeth in him should not perish but have everlasting life."*

You can have a close, eternal relationship with Him by trusting in Christ alone to save you from the curse that has fallen on all mankind. In fact, when you confess your sins and receive Him into your heart, God gives you the right to become His forgiven child: *"But as many as received him, to them he gave the power to become the sons of God, even to them who believe on his name"* (John 1:12).

This means that you can stop trying to save yourself by being "good." You don't have to face your sometimes overwhelming problems by yourself any longer. You can simply accept Jesus Christ as your only Lord and Savior. And as His child, you can call upon Him for help anytime for His forgiveness, strength, and guidance.

It really is that simple. I've seen the most skeptical hearts touched and impossibly desperate lives changed all over the world. I know it works! I have seen it happen too many times to question Christ's power to save. And the reason salvation works is because a supernatural change begins when you reach out in faith. God doesn't work as man would, by cleaning up the outside. He does it so differently that we cannot help but understand that it has to be Him, not us, who does this miraculous work of salvation.

## Change from the Inside Out

When you repent of sin and ask Jesus Christ to come inside to be your Lord and Savior, the transformation that begins is internal, first and foremost. Yet the evidence of the transformation becomes apparent externally, as well. Many of the outward things that once were so important to you simply matter less and less. You begin to love the things God loves and hate the things God hates.

When you think about it, it makes sense that all change must come from inside and are not mere external actions. We see the same pattern in the natural realm. Scientists explain that you cannot change an element unless you change its nucleus. In order for a person to change, the nucleus, or innermost self, must change first.

Knowing this, we should also realize that we cannot change ourselves simply by dealing with outward things. Too often in all areas of life we seek to transform ourselves by adjusting the external aspects of our lives: our jobs, relationships, or hobbies, thinking these changes will bring growth, happiness, and newness to our lives. Permanent or real change only comes when the center of our being, our inner drives and motivations, undergoes transformation. And only Jesus Christ can bring that kind of change. You must take the initiative to trust Jesus and to receive Him, but it is He who is able to transform you from the inside out.

How do you begin?

Revelation 3:20 sets a clear agenda: *"Behold, I stand at the door and knock; if any man hear my voice, and open the door, I will come in to him, and will sup with him, and he with me."*

This internal door-opening is also explained in Romans 10:9: *"That if thou shalt confess with thy mouth the Lord Jesus, and shalt believe in thine heart that God hath raised him from the dead, thou shalt be saved."*

## His Sacrifice, Your Salvation

Allow me to mention Mel Gibson's movie one more time. There were so many memorable scenes from *The Passion of the Christ*. Frankly, the entire two hours was a gut-wrenching testimony revealing just how much Jesus Christ was willing to plunge into the darkness of the human soul in order to purchase our redemption. Even the most simple verses in the Bible gained new meaning:

*For God so loved the world, that he gave his only begotten Son, that whosoever believeth in him should not perish, but have everlasting life. For God sent not his Son into the world to condemn the world; but that the world through him might be saved. He that believeth on him is not condemned: but he that believeth not is condemned already, because he hath not believed in the name of the only begotten Son of God.* (John 3:16-18)

One of the most unforgettable scenes for me came when Jesus painfully struggled to straighten up after being flogged with rods. The soldiers angrily reached for their glass- and metal-tipped lashes, ready to deliver more blows and flesh-piercing punishment. I wanted to cry, "Stay down. Don't take any more." Yet I knew Jesus would take more…and more. It was my sin, and your sin, that required atonement and payment. Someone had to die—the perfect Lamb of God. As many others have related, it was then that so many viewers realized that it was our hands that were swinging the lacerating lash and driving the nails into the Son of God's flesh. It was literally our own mouths mocking Him and calling for the Christ's execution.

It was for our sins. What a stunning realization! The Lamb of God went through all that for each of us. And there is no getting around this fact: *"But God commendeth his love toward us, in that, while we were yet sinners, Christ died for us"* (Romans 5:8).

As Romans 3:25 describes, *"God sent Jesus to take the punishment for our sins and to satisfy God's anger against us"* (NLT).

Dear reader, if you haven't done so already, is there any reason why you cannot receive Jesus Christ into your heart right now? If you are willing to let go of your burdens and challenges, and if you will repent of your sins and receive Jesus Christ as your Lord and Savior, you can do it right now. At this moment you can pray the most important prayer of your life. You can use words such as these:

> Lord Jesus, I've messed up my life. I know that I'm a sinner. I realize that I need your forgiveness. I believe that You died for my sins. I'm tired of being separated from You. I now invite You to come into my heart and my life. I trade my past for everything You want to give me. I trust You as my Savior, and I want to follow You and live for You. Amen!

If you prayed that prayer and meant it, the Bible has more life-changing promises for you, including the one found in Romans 10:13: "*For whoever calls upon the name of the Lord shall be saved.*"

The Bible offers this truth as well: "*Therefore if any man be in Christ, he is a new creature: old things are passed away; behold, all things are become new*" (2 Corinthians 5:17).

When you have accepted Jesus you have joined a special family—the family of God. You are part of a worldwide network that includes movie producers, presidents, royalty, businesspeople, actors, professional athletes, singers, truck drivers, computer operators, children, and lots of people who have been faced with challenges possibly even worse than yours.

And with the saints, you can sing:

On a hill far away stood an old rugged cross,
The emblem of suff'ring and shame;
And I love that old cross where the dearest and best
For a world of lost sinners was slain.

So I'll cherish the old rugged cross,
Till my trophies at last I lay down.
I will cling to the old rugged cross,
and exchange it some day for a crown.[1]

You are beginning your life in Jesus Christ now! You are taking your first steps on the greatest adventure you can ever imagine. The blood of the Lamb has been applied to your life, and your own Passover has begun. You now have a personal relationship with God, a relationship that is eternal and unlike anything you have ever known. As your relationship grows from day to day, and as you get to know Him better, you will come to love Him more and more.

Now, more than ever, you are ready to unleash your Passover blessings!

# CHAPTER 12

# UNLEASHING
# YOUR BLESSINGS

THE PASSOVER WAS INCREDIBLY IMPORTANT to the children of Israel, for it determined their future as it protected their nation and future generations from certain extinction. It is no wonder that people of Jewish heritage celebrate it even today.

Likewise, as with Passover and the children of Israel, the Lamb of God allows us to pass from death to life, and from sin's slavery to eternal freedom. In Exodus 12:11-13 we read:

*And thus shall ye eat it; with your loins girded, your shoes on your feet, and your staff in your hand; and ye shall eat it in haste: it is the LORD's passover. For I will pass through the land of Egypt this night, and will smite all the firstborn in the land of Egypt, both man and beast; and against all the gods of Egypt I will execute judgment: I am the LORD. And the blood shall be to you for a token upon the houses where ye are: and when I see the blood, I will pass over you, and the plague shall not be upon you to destroy you, when I smite the land of Egypt.*

Now read Romans 3:24-25:

*They receive God's approval freely by an act of his kindness through the price Christ Jesus paid to set us free [from sin]. God showed that Christ is the throne of mercy where God's approval is given through faith in Christ's blood. In his patience God waited to deal with sins committed in the past.* (GW)

Now that we are free from our sins because of Christ's blood, we have been given the liberty to enjoy the blessings of both the Old and New Covenants, specifically the seven blessings of the Passover.

## Seven Blessings

Let's look back at Exodus 23, a very revealing passage of Scripture and one that Christians have ignored for too long. It focuses on the feasts of the Passover season, and in this passage are seven specific blessings of the Passover (all references NKJV):

1. **God will assign an angel to you**—*"Behold, I send an Angel before you to keep you in the way and to bring you into the place which I have prepared"* (verse 20); and *"For My Angel will go before you"* (verse 23).

2. **God will be an enemy to your enemies**—*"But if you indeed obey His voice and do all that I speak, then I will be an enemy to your enemies and an adversary to your adversaries"* (verse 22).

3. **God will give you prosperity**—*"So you shall serve the LORD your God, and He will bless your bread and your water"* (verse 25).

4. **God will take sickness away from you**—*"And I will take sickness away from the midst of you"* (verse 25).

5. **God will give you a long life**—*"No one shall suffer miscarriage or be barren in your land; I will fulfill the number of your days"* (verse 26).

6. **God will bring increase and inheritance**—*"Little by little I will drive them out from before you, until you have increased, and you inherit the land"* (verse 30).

7. **God will give a special year of blessing**—*"And I will set your bounds from the Red Sea to the sea, Philistia, and from the desert to the River. For I*

*will deliver the inhabitants of the land into your hand, and you shall drive them out before you*" (verse 31); and what the enemy stole will be returned to you and protected by God from being overtaken: "*I will not drive them out from before you in one year, lest the land become desolate and the beast of the field become too numerous for you*" (verse 29).

These Passover season blessings are very specific and astounding, which is why I spent an entire chapter on each blessing. Now I want to narrow everything down to three focused areas in which you can begin to unleash these blessings in your life.

## Unleash God's Plan for Your Life

Be willing to dig deeper, sacrifice more, and grow stronger than you've ever dreamed. Let me illustrate. At almost every county fair, carnival, and fun park, you see children and their parents on carousels. It seems that everyone loves to ride the festively painted horses, swans, and other figurines. Have you noticed, though, that there comes a time when boys and girls start realizing that going around in circles is baby stuff? Suddenly, at a certain age, the young people want to do other things at the carnival that are more challenging.

I've often wondered why so many believers in the Lamb of God are content to ride throughout life on spiritual carousels. Too often we fall at the foot of the Cross and accept Jesus Christ as Savior, then we look around, see an apparently happy group going around in circles, figure God must be in the center of it, and ride along. Sadly, it gets easier and easier to just go around in circles, never really understanding that the path from the cross of Calvary to God's throne room in heaven is often a rugged road.

The message of the Cross, plain and simple, comes directly from the words of the Savior:

*Then said Jesus unto his disciples, If any man will come after me, let him deny himself, and take up his cross, and follow me. For whosoever will save his life shall lose it: and whosoever will lose his life for my sake shall find it. For what is a man profited, if he shall gain the whole world, and lose his own soul? or what shall a man give in exchange for his soul? For the Son of man shall come in the glory of his Father with his angels; and then he shall reward every man according to his works.* (Matthew 16:24-27)

Throughout the pages of this book I've shared how the Cross stands at the central point in history's time line. From the Old Testament feasts, especially Passover, Jesus Christ is the focus of all Scripture. Jesus Christ came to die for mankind's sins, yet He came, first and foremost, to restore His children to a life of fellowship with the Father. Understanding the message that we must unleash God's will as we take up our cross and follow Him is absolutely necessary to developing a walk of close fellowship and supernatural blessings. It is also vital to understanding that our steps today are preparation for a lifetime in eternity with the Savior.

So, what does it mean to unleash God's plan for your life, to embrace the cross, to take it up and follow Him? What was Jesus telling us to do?

Let's go to the core of following Christ. I believe this is a much-needed message that God's people desperately need. The apostle Paul wrote about this need in his Holy Spirit–inspired letter to the church in Rome:

*What shall we say then? Shall we continue in sin, that grace may abound? God forbid. How shall we, that are dead to sin, live any longer therein? Know ye not, that so many of us as were baptized into Jesus Christ were baptized into his death? Therefore we are buried with him by baptism into death: that like as Christ was raised up from the dead by the glory of the Father, even so we also should walk in newness of life.*

*For if we have been planted together in the likeness of his death, we shall be also in the likeness of his resurrection: Knowing this, that our old man is crucified with him, that the body of sin might be destroyed, that henceforth we should not serve sin. For he that is dead is freed from sin. Now if we be dead with Christ, we believe that we shall also live with him: Knowing that Christ being raised from the dead dieth no more; death hath no more dominion over him. For in that he died, he died unto sin once: but in that he liveth, he liveth unto God.* (Romans 6:1-10)

What we've just read has become almost foreign in the lives of too many buffet-type Christians: "I'll have a lot of grace, a bite or two of faith, and a little dab of concern, but none of that self-sacrifice! We hear so little about sanctification, so seldom on living the holy life. For too long we've talked about the Christian life in terms of having a wonderful life, of finally having more meaning, of finding fulfillment, and of eventually going to heaven. All those are good, but they don't reflect what following Christ truly involves.

Jesus spoke of this in John 12:24-26, as He taught this mighty parable:

*Verily, verily, I say unto you, Except a corn of wheat fall into the ground and die, it abideth alone: but if it die, it bringeth forth much fruit. He that loveth his life shall lose it; and he that hateth his life in this world shall keep it unto life eternal. If any man serve me, let him follow me; and where I am, there shall also my servant be: if any man serve me, him will my Father honour.*

What a picture! In the parable of the seed, Jesus ties serving Him and self-sacrifice together. The irony of the abundant, super-natural life is that it involves death to self. The decision must be made continually. Following Christ means unleashing Him to work in you every day by embracing the cross and accepting the changes that He brings.

## Unleash Your Faith

Nothing miraculous happens without faith. Until Moses stretched the rod over the Red Sea, the water stayed intact. Until David unleashed the small stone from his sling, Goliath towered over him, sneering at the young man's God.

Think about the faith that it took for blind Bartimaeus to cry out to the Lord, *"Have mercy on me."* Those around him were most likely discomforted by his yelling, and they may have even told him to be quiet. Nevertheless, he kept shouting out, *"Jesus, thou son of David, have mercy on me"* (Luke 18:38). What was Bartimaeus doing? He was acting upon his faith, and he got his answer.

Another example was the woman with the issue of blood. Her faith was so remarkable that her miracle is recorded in Matthew 9, Mark 5, and Luke 8. She said, *"If I may but touch his garment, I'll be whole."* She reached out for her answer, the Lord Jesus, and she was healed. Jesus even spoke about her actions that brought restoration: *"Thy faith hath made thee whole"* (Matthew 9:22).

The early church is another example of faith in action. On the Day of Pentecost *"they were all filled with the Holy Ghost, and began to speak with other tongues, as the Spirit gave them utterance"* (Acts 2:4). Believers prayed and then began to speak, acting upon the revelation and infilling that God had given them. Like the early church, we must not wait and then react, but rather act first in faith and then see God move. You see, pursuit is faith in action: *"Without faith it is impossible to please him: for he that cometh to God must believe that he is, and that he is a rewarder of them that diligently seek him"* (Hebrews 11:6).

Your unleashed faith brings victory!

## Unleash Your Courage

Can you imagine what it was like for the children of Israel as they realized they were trapped, upwards to 3 million strong, between drowning in the Red Sea and being slain by the Pharoah's army?

They had been faithful in observing the Passover. The long-anticipated exodus from Egypt happened. Then, when things seemed to be going so well, they were at the place of no return. They were either going to see another unthinkable miracle of legendary proportions or they were going to die at the hands of Egyptians, who were undoubtedly bloodthirsty after enduring the ten plagues!

Yet because they had been faithful in honoring God's direction concerning the Passover, and because they were God's chosen people, He worked a mighty miracle:

*And when Pharaoh drew nigh, the children of Israel lifted up their eyes, and, behold, the Egyptians marched after them; and they were sore afraid: and the children of Israel cried out unto the LORD. . . .*

*And the LORD said unto Moses, Wherefore criest thou unto me? speak unto the children of Israel, that they go forward: But lift thou up thy rod, and stretch out thine hand over the sea, and divide it: and the children of Israel shall go on dry ground through the midst of the sea. . . .*

*And the children of Israel went into the midst of the sea upon the dry ground: and the waters were a wall unto them on their right hand, and on their left. . . .*

*And Moses stretched forth his hand over the sea, and the sea returned to his strength when the morning appeared; and the Egyptians fled against it; and the LORD overthrew the Egyptians in the midst of the sea. . . .*

*Thus the LORD saved Israel that day out of the hand of the Egyptians; and Israel saw the Egyptians dead upon the sea shore.*

*And Israel saw that great work which the LORD did upon the Egyptians: and the people feared the LORD, and believed the LORD, and his servant Moses.* (Exodus 14:10, 15-16, 22, 27, 30-31)

Cecil B. DeMille, even with today's movie-making technology, could never do this miraculous scene as it actually happened. Can you imagine? In the midst of the horrifying desperation and impending doom, God gave calmness. He told the children of Israel not to be afraid and to go forward. Oh, that we could learn the lessons of the victory God wants to give us when we are obedient and faithful.

It's time that we unleashed our faith! The church is engaged in a war, and you cannot be victorious if you do not accept your place as a conquering soldier and fight. It is every Christian's job to be a faith-filled soldier of the kingdom of God, a soldier of the cross.

The insightful Bible teacher E. M. Bounds once wrote:

We are not imaginary soldiers fighting an imaginary war—all is real and true. Because he is truthful, a girded soldier is strong, prepared, and intense in his fight. Truth is the ornament of a jeweled belt, a diamond set in gold. We must conquer the devil by truth as the strength and support of our lives. We know the truth and have the truth because we have Christ who is the truth.[1]

It is vital to your success in this life as a Christian that you lay aside the cares of this world and keep heaven's purpose on your mind. Second Timothy 2:4 states, *"No man that warreth entangleth himself with the affairs of this life; that he may please him who hath chosen him to be a soldier."*

You have been chosen to be a part of God's holy army. In order to fight the good fight you must lay aside the weights that hold you back from receiving the blessings the Father has intended for you.

God has promised you power to subdue your enemies and recover your losses. The book of Revelation trumpets: *"They overcame him by the blood of the Lamb"* (12:11). God has already made you an overcomer as a blood-bought believer, so do not hide or be reluctant to battle because of fear. Unleash your courage. Be full of faith as you activate God's promises in your life.

Psalm 108:13 says, *"Through God we shall do valiantly: for he it is that shall tread down our enemies."* God's Word declares that you shall do "valiantly," but it is impossible to succeed in our own ability. Philippians 4:13 says, *"I can do all things through Christ which strengtheneth me."* The key to unleashing your courage is to remain under the blood of the Lamb. As you do, God will go with you and help you, strengthening you for your journey.

The people who place their trust in God accomplish great things for the kingdom. Daniel 11:32 says that you will be strong and *"do exploits."* Whatever enemy and obstacle has held you back, stolen from you, and caused you sorrow must flee away in the name of Jesus.

Dwight L. Moody said, "When a battle is fought, all are anxious to know who the victors are.[2] First John 5:4-5 says, *"For whatsoever is born of God overcometh the world: and this is the victory that overcometh the world, even our faith. Who is he that overcometh the world, but he that believeth that Jesus is the Son of God?"* These verses tell us who is to gain victory in life.

The believer gains victory by unleashing courage! May the Holy Ghost put fire in your soul so you may stand in faith upon the promises in God's Word and, being sufficient in all things, you may rest assured that you will live blessed as God has intended.

## Unleash Your Finances

Notice that in the Exodus 23 passage used throughout this book there is a prerequisite to all these blessings 5 as the children of

Israel were given instructions for the Passover season: *"None shall appear before me empty"* (verse 15).

Granted, the children of Israel were required to bring more than twenty different offerings to the Lord, both great and small. During the Passover season, however, the offering was unique by promising seven specific blessings.

That should settle it, once and for all. This Passover offering should not be confused with the tithe or other offerings throughout the year. God says, *"Thou shalt not delay to offer the first of thy ripe fruits"* (Exodus 22:29). The Feast of Firstfruits is part of the Passover season. The lesson is clear. The Israelites were leaving Egypt after more than four centuries of slavery. God was preparing to kill all the firstborn of Egypt as the last of the ten plagues because Pharaoh would not let His people go. In other words, the Egyptians would not give, so God took from them. On the other hand, the children of Israel gave in obedience, so God blessed them beyond measure.

Referring to the Passover and firstfruits offering, God told Moses: *"So this [festival] will be [like] a mark on your hand and [like] a band on your forehead, because the LORD used his mighty hand to bring us out of Egypt"* (Exodus 13:16, GW). It was a reminder that the Lord had brought them out of bondage with great power!

What are your firstfruits? For starters, 2 Corinthians 8:2-5 makes one thing very clear:

> *How that in a great trial of affliction the abundance of their joy and their deep poverty abounded unto the riches of their liberality. For to their power, I bear record, yea, and beyond their power they were willing of themselves; Praying us with much intreaty that we would receive the gift, and take upon us the fellowship of the ministering to the saints. And this they did, not as we hoped, but first gave their own selves to the Lord, and unto us by the will of God.*

The important sentence is this: *"But first gave their own selves to the Lord."* What is the first thing we have to give to the Lord? Not our money, but ourselves. That is how it must begin with each of us. Do not give your money to God if you have not given yourself. You cannot buy a personal relationship with God. God can get along without your money. It is for your benefit that God requires you to give, but He has an order. He wants you first. Then, out of the giving of yourself, the other blessings will follow.

Beyond yourself, your firstfruits should be a special offering, not your tithe or a "normal" offering. It should be sacrificial. In Bible times it was the first lamb from each mother sheep, which represented a major investment and the "loss" of future generations of lambs. To us in a nonrural environment, it can be the firstfruits of anything that God supplies to us in many ways.

How much should it be worth? Only God can reveal that to you. Ask Him. I know from personal experience that He will give you the amount. Whatever it is, it should be worthy to commemorate what He has done for you through His shed blood: *"Honour the Lord with thy substance, and with the firstfruits of all thine increase: So shall thy barns be filled with plenty, and thy presses shall burst out with new wine"* (Proverbs 3:9-10).

God will multiply your special offering back in supernatural ways. How do I know that? Luke 6:38 promises, *"Give, and it shall be given unto you; good measure, pressed down, and shaken together, and running over, shall men give into your bosom. For with the same measure that ye mete withal it shall be measured to you again."*

God has a wonderful plan for your financial future. The Bible is filled with promises of the Father's blessings for those who understand and obey the Creator's fixed laws of sowing and reaping. As you apply His kingdom principles, you can live an abundant life that is filled with financial miracles!

From the beginning, God made provision for every need of mankind. At Creation, He commanded the earth to produce and bring forth a harvest (Genesis 1:11). When God created Adam, He gave Adam every seed to produce his food (Genesis 1:29), instructing him to eat the fruit and not the seed.

God has already given you and me everything we need— everything we need to meet our needs, everything we need to get out of debt, and everything we need to preach the Gospel. And it is all on earth right now! Therefore, each of us must address the real question: How do I access what God has already given me? The answer is in the seed you have been given to sow.

It is a fixed law: The earth must produce when a seed is sown. When God said, *"Let the earth bring forth"* (Genesis 1:11), He gave the command for multiplication, but He gave the seed to man. The earth has been commanded to produce, and when seed is sown, the harvest yields seed and fruit *"after his kind"* (Genesis 1:12). Becoming a knowledgeable and diligent sower is a vital key to your harvest: You could have all the seed sitting in your hand, and it will never bring forth a harvest if it is not sown.

What has God put into your hand? According to God's Word, He provides seed to the sower. The Word of God declares in 2 Corinthians 9:10, *"Now he that ministereth seed to the sower both minister bread for your food, and multiply your seed sown, and increase the fruits of your righteousness."*

Why does God want to bless you so much? There is coming a supernatural harvest unlike anything we have ever seen before. It is a harvest of ideas, creativity, inventions, talents, expansion, and influence. It is a spiritual harvest of miracles and souls as well as a vast harvest of financial blessings. Increasingly, *"the wealth of the sinner"* is increasingly being *"stored up for the righteous"* (Proverbs 13:22, NKJV). And you can be part of it!

I want your life to abound with God's blessings (Proverbs 28:20). I want you to experience God's boundless provision to *"supply all your need according to his riches in glory by Christ Jesus"* (Philippians 4:19) and the "no lack blessings" promised in the Word of God, *"always having all sufficiency in all things"* (2 Corinthians 9:8).

Why is this coming supernatural harvest so vital? I am fully convinced that God desires to bestow financial blessing to people who will generously support His work and help carry the message of His Son to the world.

In Matthew 24 when Jesus was asked about the last days, He said: *"And this gospel of the kingdom shall be preached in all the world for a witness unto all nations; and then shall the end come"* (verse 14). We are coming closer and closer to the time of the Lord's return. Yet in the midst of some of the most uncertain and perilous times our world has known, God is opening unimaginable doors to the Gospel. What happens next, I believe, will be a direct result of how believers respond to the coming supernatural harvest through the seed they sow, especially through the Passover offering.

Unleashing your finances during the coming days is directly related to obeying God's laws of giving. God's divine design for your financial success will not happen without your cooperation! The release of God's blessings in your life is connected to your obedience, for the Bible declares: *"And all these blessings shall come on thee, and overtake thee, if thou shalt hearken unto the voice of the LORD thy God"* (Deuteronomy 28:2).

Sowing always precedes reaping, and seed time always precedes harvest. The seed you sow today in faith will produce a harvest of abundance and blessings on your life and will take the Gospel message of Jesus Christ to the nations of the world.

God has a divine plan for your financial success! These timeless keys are revealed throughout the Bible, and they are given to help you implement God's plan and to help you succeed in everything you do!

## A Final Note

God does not give the seven blessings of the Passover lightly. There is a purpose much larger than for you or me. The reason for a supernatural outpouring of blessings related to the Passover is very clear: The greatest commission and calling as believers in Jesus Christ is to take the mighty message of the Gospel into all the earth. We are to share it with all nations, *"baptizing them in the name of the Father, and of the Son and of the Holy Ghost"* (Matthew 28:19), and teaching them to observe the Lord's commandments.

I love what Dr. Billy Graham has said: "My one purpose in life is to help people find a personal relationship with God, which, I believe, comes through knowing Christ."[3] He certainly took Christ at His word, especially the Word found in Mark 16:15, *"Go ye into all the world and preach the gospel to every creature."*

As Corrie ten Boom often said, "Everyone is either a missionary or a mission field."[4] Once we are born again, it becomes our job and calling to reach people with the Gospel and build them up in the knowledge of the Lord. The Lord promised to go with you as you spread His Word. He stands right there with you, backing you up as you enforce His victory.

Matthew 28:20 says, *"I am with you alway, even unto the end of the world."* The Lord Jesus is counting on you and me to do go and tell others about His love, for the Lord knows that when His church truly fulfills the Great Commission, a powerful move of God will come.

Revelation 12:11 says, *"And they overcame him by the blood of the Lamb, and by the word of their testimony; and they loved not their lives unto the death."*

God is moving mightily today. He is shaking the nations. We have a great work to do. He has promised to supply whatever we need to accomplish all that He has called us to do:

*Verily, verily, I say unto you, He that believeth on me, the works that I do shall he do also; and greater works than these shall he do; because I go unto my Father. And whatsoever ye shall ask in my name, that will I do, that the Father may be glorified in the Son. If ye shall ask any thing in my name, I will do it.* (John 14:12-14)

My heartfelt prayer is this: May the Lamb of God bless you richly in all that you do for Him in the days to come: *"Now unto him that is able to do exceeding abundantly above all that we ask or think, according to the power that worketh in us, unto him be glory in the church by Christ Jesus throughout all ages, world without end. Amen"* (Ephesians 3:20-21).

I look forward to rejoicing with you in heaven for all that the Lamb of God accomplishes through you as a result of the unleashed Passover blessings in your life!

# NOTES

Introduction
1. Dr. Eugene H. Merrill, *An Historical Survey of the Old Testament* (Nutley, NJ: Craig Press, 1966), 102.

Chapter 1
1. For a detailed teaching on the seven feasts, read Benny Hinn's insightful book, *Lamb of God: Yesterday, Today & Forever* (Dallas: Clarion Call Marketing, Inc., 2004).

Chapter 2
1. John G. Foote, "When I See the Blood," (nineteenth century).

Chapter 4
1. Lester Sumrall, *Angels: The Messengers of God* (South Bend, IN: Sumrall Publishing, reprint 2004), n.p.
2. John Calvin, *Institutes of the Christian Religion* (Book 1), Translated from Latin by Henry Beveridge, Esq. (London: Bonham Norton, 1599), chapter 14, section 6.
3. Dr. Billy Graham, *Angels: God's Secret Agents* (Nashville: W Publishing Group, 1995), 241–42.
4. Graham, *Angels*, 30.
5. *The New Unger's Bible Dictionary* (Personal Computer Study Bible; originally published in hardcopy by Chicago's Moody Press in 1988).
6. Sumrall, *Angels*, 5.

Chapter 5
1. E. M. Bounds, *Guide to Spiritual Warfare* (New Kensington, PA: Whitaker House, 1984), 25–26.

2. Charles Spurgeon, *Spurgeon on Prayer and Spiritual Warfare* (New Kensington, PA: Whitaker House, 1998), 543.

Chapter 7
1. A. W. Tozer, *The Tozer Pulpit Set,* volume 1, book 1 (Camp Hill, PA: Christian Publications, 1994), 34.

Chapter 8
1. Bill Gaither, "The Longer I Serve Him," copyright 1965 by William J. Gaither. All rights reserved. International copyright secured. Used by permission.

Chapter 9
1. D. L. Moody, as quoted in W. R. Moody, *The Life of D. L. Moody* (New York, Fleming H. Revell, 1900), 149.
2. Smith Wigglesworth, *Smith Wigglesworth on Faith* (New Kensington, PA: Whitaker House, 1998), 135–36.
3. Wigglesworth, *Wigglesworth on Faith*, 189.

Chapter 10
1. Charles Finney, *The Spirit-Filled Life* (New Kensington, PA: Whitaker House, 1999), 117.

Chapter 11
1. George Bennard, "The Old Rugged Cross," copyright ©1913 by George Bennard. Renewed 1951 by the Rodeheaver (a division of Word, Inc.). All rights reserved. International copyright secured. Used by permission.

Chapter 12
1. E. M. Bounds, *Guide to Spiritual Warfare* (New Kensington, PA: Whitaker House, 1984), 148.

2. Dwight L. Moody, *Your Victory in Jesus* (New Kensington, PA: Whitaker House, 1995), 8.

3. Dr. Billy Graham, www.billygraham.org.

4. Corrie ten Boom, *Messages of God's Abundance* (Grand Rapids, MI: Zondervan, 2002), 47.